The (Un)Written Constitution

The (Un)Written Constitution

GEORGE THOMAS

OXFORD
UNIVERSITY PRESS

Oxford University Press is a department of the University of Oxford. It furthers
the University's objective of excellence in research, scholarship, and education
by publishing worldwide. Oxford is a registered trade mark of Oxford University
Press in the UK and certain other countries.

Published in the United States of America by Oxford University Press
198 Madison Avenue, New York, NY 10016, United States of America.

Library of Congress Cataloging-in-Publication Data
Names: Thomas, George, 1970- author.
Title: The (un)written constitution / George Thomas.
Other titles: Unwritten constitution
Description: New York, NY : Oxford University Press, [2021] | Includes
bibliographical references and index.
Identifiers: LCCN 2021009029 (print) | LCCN 2021009030 (ebook) |
ISBN 9780197555972 (hardback) | ISBN 9780197555996 (epub)
Subjects: LCSH: Constitutional law—United States.
Classification: LCC KF4550 .T46 2021 (print) | LCC KF4550 (ebook) |
DDC 342.73/001–dc23
LC record available at https://lccn.loc.gov/2021009029
LC ebook record available at https://lccn.loc.gov/2021009030

DOI: 10.1093/oso/9780197555972.001.0001

1 3 5 7 9 8 6 4 2

Printed by Sheridan Books, Inc., United States of America

For Courtney, Ange, and Izzy

Contents

Introduction

Interpreting a Written Constitution

> For that matter, maybe we can just for a second talk about
> the arcane matter, the Constitution.
>
> —Justice Neil Gorsuch

> The use of words is to express ideas . . . But no language
> is so copious as to supply words and phrases for every
> complex idea, or so correct as not to include many
> equivocally denoting different ideas.
>
> —James Madison

Like a teacher admonishing his students to return to the subject at hand, Justice Neil Gorsuch urged counsel arguing before the Supreme Court—and, implicitly, his fellow justices—to return to the Constitution. It's a refrain we hear often enough in constitutional debate. One side wants to stick to the Constitution, while the other side strays to questions of politics, policy, morality, or philosophy. To things that are not properly part of the Constitution. So much so, according to Justice Gorsuch, that much of constitutional law has rendered the written Constitution "arcane"—that is, obscure or mysterious. Gorsuch was being ironic, but his meaning was exquisitely clear: The Constitution is not a mystery. And it is the Constitution we are interpreting.

Yet was this truly in dispute?

This particular oral argument concerned whether partisan gerrymandering—that is, drawing the boundaries of districts to favor a particular political party—could be so extreme as to be

The (Un)Written Constitution. George Thomas, Oxford University Press. © Oxford University Press 2021.
DOI: 10.1093/oso/9780197555972.003.0001

unconstitutional. Justice Gorsuch's quite legitimate concern was whether the text of the Constitution provided any justification for *the judiciary* to make such a constitutional judgment. He pointed to a number of textual provisions in the Constitution that authorized the Congress to intervene in the process of a state's voting procedures.[1] But nothing in these particular textual provisions seemed to authorize *courts* to find partisan gerrymandering unconstitutional. What discernable constitutional standard could courts apply to this case? Justice Gorsuch wondered if counsel was, in essence, trying to argue that partisan gerrymandering could so distort political representation that it essentially violated Article IV's promise that the "United States shall guarantee to every State in this Union a Republican Form of Government." Like other textual provisions that invited Congress to intervene in state electoral rules—the Fifteenth, Nineteenth, Twenty-Fourth, and Twenty-Sixth Amendments in particular—this clause suggested a legislative remedy, not judicial relief. Without a clear textual standard to guide courts, Justice Gorsuch worried that the judiciary was being invited to act like a legislature.

There was such a standard, the lawyer making the case responded. It was supplied by the First Amendment's rights of political speech and association and the Fourteenth Amendment's guarantee of equal protection; previous courts had relied on these standards to provide judicial relief. At just this moment, Justice Ruth Bader Ginsburg interrupted, asking where our notion of "one person, one vote" came from.[2] Her point was obvious: It came from the equal protection clause of the Fourteenth Amendment, giving the complaint clear footing in constitutional text.

Was one of these justices engaged in *constitutional* interpretation and the other not?

Justice Gorsuch's concern was that "a generic equal protection claim" is far too abstract a standard to give the judiciary clear constitutional guidance in finding that a state has impermissibly diluted the vote of some of its citizens by drawing voting districts on the basis of partisan identity. Without clear and discernable standards derived from constitutional text, the Supreme Court would intrude into legislative terrain. It's not simply that such questions are best left to the legislature. Without judicially discernable standards these arguments invite "judges to behave like legislators, imposing their moral convictions and utility calculi on others."[3] Justice Gorsuch may well be right. And yet, if he is, it is largely because of his underlying understanding of the functions, powers, and obligations of the different branches of government within the separation of powers. His argument is derived from the *unwritten* logic of the separation of powers.[4] It is rooted in such *unwritten* understandings every bit as much as Justice Ginsburg's argument that partisan gerrymandering might violate the equality of citizens by weighing some of their votes more than others—thus distorting the democratic process by privileging some citizens over others for partisan reasons in violation of the equal protection clause of the Fourteenth Amendment.

Both justices root their arguments in constitutional text. But both justices also situate the text in terms of larger constitutional understandings that are not textually explicit. The real quarrel between these justices was how best to understand the unwritten Constitution. Justice Ginsburg depends on some unwritten standard of what democracy requires with regard to equal representation, but so, too, does Justice Gorsuch depend on some unwritten standard of what the separation of powers requires in a democracy. They are both engaged in an effort to faithfully interpret the Constitution. To do so, they must rest their textual readings on unwritten ideas that are an inescapable feature of constitutional interpretation. And the debate between them, like many of our most pressing constitutional debates, is a debate about which unwritten understandings and principles should guide our reading of constitutional text.

This is the central claim of *The (Un)Written Constitution*. This book seeks, first, to make visible the unwritten ideas and understandings that good faith efforts to interpret the Constitution rest on. Second, it illustrates how our central constitutional debates, which have been with us from the beginning, are debates about unwritten ideas and understandings.[5] This is true of even the most scrupulous textualists. It is true of the late Justice Antonin Scalia. The defining feature of Scalia's thinking is his insistence on interpreting constitutional text based on the original understanding of those who ratified it. To do otherwise is to indulge a "living constitution" that changes and evolves based on current understandings, rendering the written Constitution "useless." This sentiment has come to frame public debate about constitutional interpretation and especially discourse on the Supreme Court. Consider Justice Gorsuch's comments earlier: When we look beyond the text, we are inescapably looking to our own political preferences. Praising Justice Scalia during his confirmation hearings, Justice Brett Kavanaugh frequently turned to his well-thumbed pocket Constitution to suggest that *either* we are interpreting the precise text of the Constitution *or* we are going beyond interpretation and basing our judgments on the best policy.[6] Justice Amy Coney Barrett, a former law clerk to Justice Scalia, also insisted at her confirmation hearings that Scalia's jurisprudence was her own.

Yet the very nature of a written constitution requires us to interpret the written text based on its underlying ideas. Not because we are trying to rewrite the Constitution to make it accord with our policy preferences, but because the text does not explain itself. The meaning and significance of a *written* constitution is itself the subject of debate.[7] In Federalist 37, which supplies one of the epigraphs to the Introduction, Madison pointed to the limits of language in conveying complex ideas and concepts by way of a written text given the "complexity and novelty of the objects defined."[8] Moving beyond the text is an inescapable feature of *interpreting* the written Constitution. This is just as true for so-called textualists as it is for everyone else. Thomas Reed Powell famously advised his law students at Harvard not to read the Constitution because it would only confuse them. That's misguided. Constitutional text is the place to begin; it is, after all, what we are interpreting. It frames our constitutional disputes and provides a common ground that all may look to. We owe a debt to textualists like Justice Scalia for persistently making this point. Yet it's equally misguided to think that reading the Constitution alone will answer our most pressing constitutional questions. To make sense of text, we must go beyond text.[9] The Constitution cannot be understood apart from the ideas and principles it sits atop. Much of our real disagreement regarding the Constitution resides in our debates over these unwritten ideas and principles.

Yes, sometimes the text is exquisitely clear. Article II instructs us that the president must be 35 years of age and serve for four years. There is no need to move beyond the text to understand the constitutional command in this case. But we also come to text that gives Congress the power the power to "declare War," along with text that vests the "executive Power" in the president and makes the president "Commander in Chief of the Army and Navy." How do we determine whether Congress's power to initiate war is exclusive or precisely what the executive power includes? What about the Fourteenth Amendment's command that no state shall deny any person of the equal protection of the laws? For example, Justice Scalia was absolutely certain that the Fourteenth Amendment's promise that "no state shall deny any person the equal protection of the laws" forbids states from prohibiting interracial marriage, but he was equally certain that this textual provision does not bar states from prohibiting same-sex marriage. Why? Constitutional text says nothing about either. How we apply the text to these particular cases turns on unwritten understandings that bring constitutional text to life.

There's nothing unusual about this; it's hardly news to scholarly defenders of originalism.[10] Yet this point is obscured by the most prominent *judicial* advocates of textualism. There is a disjunction between the public face of textualism and originalism—where unwritten understandings are frequently denied or simply merged with text—and the sophisticated scholarship that has grown up around originalism where unwritten understandings are not only acknowledged but are also a powerful feature of originalist theory.[11] As constitutional issues have become a more visible part of our ordinary politics, it's crucial that we have a better sense of how the unwritten Constitution shapes our understanding of the written Constitution—whether we are "strict constructionists," "living constitutionalists," or, more likely, something in between. Can the president fire a special counsel tasked with investigating possible violations of law by the president? Can a sitting president be indicted? Can a president pardon herself? Can Congress delegate its power to the president? On what grounds can Congress impeach a president? Can Congress impeach on officer and prohibit them from holding any office of public trust *after* they have left office?[12] Can the Supreme Court hear a case regarding what constitutes "high crimes and misdemeanors"? These pressing constitutional disputes turn on unwritten understandings. So, too, do foundational concepts and principles that we have long taken for granted. The power of the Supreme Court to find laws unconstitutional turns on unwritten concepts and understandings. Our recurrent debates in the American constitutional tradition are about the best understanding of unwritten ideas and principles—about, we might say, the best understanding of the political theory that underlies the Constitution.

With this in mind, consider an excellent suggestion from Justice Kavanaugh in an essay insisting on the *precise text* of the Constitution: "Every time we re-read the text of the Constitution, which we should do regularly—and I mean word for word—we should also re-read *Marbury v. Madison* (1803), the case where the Court articulated and first exercised the power of judicial review. For that case has profound lessons to this day about the status of the Constitution, how to interpret the Constitution and the Judiciary's role vis-à-vis other branches in interpreting the Constitution."[13] Take this advice. Read the text of the Constitution—word for word as Justice Kavanaugh says—as you read, perhaps for the first time, *Marbury v. Madison*. If you do, you'll immediately notice that when Chief Justice Marshall gets to the argument justifying judicial review, the central logic of his argument is rooted in *unwritten assumptions* about the nature of the written Constitution. Marshall's argument is rooted in, to borrow Alexander Hamilton's words from Federalist 78, the "nature and reason of the thing."[14] It is rooted in *a political theory of written constitutions*; it is this theory that guides Marshall's understanding of text. Marshall argues that "all those who have framed written constitutions contemplate them as forming the fundamental and paramount law of the nation, and consequently the theory of every such government must be, that an act of the legislature repugnant to the constitution is void." As Marshall insists, this "theory is essentially attached to a written constitution, and is consequently to be considered by this court as one of the fundamental principles of our society."[15] The written Constitution rests on a *theory*—a set of unwritten understandings—that we must treat as one of the fundamental principles of American society: The Constitution must control ordinary laws passed by the legislature.

But do courts have the power to declare ordinary laws unconstitutional? Marshall concludes that courts must have this power: "If the courts are to regard the constitution, and the constitution is superior to any ordinary act of the legislature; the constitution, and not such ordinary act, must govern the case to which they both apply." To do otherwise, Marshall argues, to refuse to allow the courts to declare acts of the legislature void if they go against the Constitution, "would subvert the very foundation of all written constitutions."[16] The crux of Marshall's argument for judicial review turns on his unwritten theory; he does not even cite constitutional text for his central contentions. Those who rejected Marshall's argument for judicial review denied his theory. Judge John Bannister Gibson, chief justice of the Supreme Court of Pennsylvania, argued that as fundamental law, the Constitution did not "come before the court." Gibson's argument, like Marshall's, rested on a *theory of a written constitution*, which he understood to be enforced by the sovereign people, not the judiciary: "I am of the opinion that it rests with the people, in whom full and absolute sovereign power resides, to correct abuses in legislation, by instructing their representatives to repeal the obnoxious act."[17] This dispute over judicial review turned on the political theory that underlies the written Constitution.

Having made the foundational argument from unwritten principles and ideas, Marshall did turn to the "peculiar expressions of the constitution of the United States" to "furnish additional arguments in favor" of his overarching analysis. Note Marshall considers these textual bits of evidence supplemental to his logical and theoretical arguments that are primary. He reads the text in light of his theory. Marshall turns to Article III's insistence that "the judicial power of the United States is extended to all cases arising under the constitution." Marshall then asks, could it "be the intention of those who gave this power, to say that, in using it, the constitution should not be looked into?" That a case before the Court arising under the Constitution should be decided without "examining the instrument under which it arises?" This, Marshall concludes, "is too extravagant to be maintained."[18] Yet to reach this resounding conclusion, we first need to accept his *theory of a written constitution*. Judge Gibson denied Marshall's theory. Gibson argued that as fundamental law the written Constitution was enforced by the people through the democratic process. In his reading, the textual provisions of Article III that spoke to "cases arising under the Constitution" referred to disputes about ordinary law. Nothing in the text invited the *extraordinary* power of judicial review. For the

Supreme Court to claim such an extraordinary power, Gibson argued, the text of the Constitution would have to clearly and explicitly grant it. Like it grants the president the power to veto legislation. But because the Constitution did not clearly grant such a power, Gibson denied that as fundamental law the written Constitution could be adjudicated by ordinary courts of law—including the Supreme Court. Marshall and Gibson both read the text based on their theory of the written constitution.[19]

Justice Kavanaugh insists that in deciding these issues, the Marshall Court focused on the "precise words of the constitutional text. It did not seek to find the best policy." Nor did it ask "what [is] the best way to do things." Kavanaugh is altogether right that Marshall did not ask about the best policy or the best way to do things. We can agree that courts should not be deciding constitutional cases by asking "what's the best policy?"[20] Here again we have the suggestion that *either* we are interpreting based on the text of the Constitution *or* we are going beyond interpretation and basing our judgments on the best policy or the best way to do things. Yet Marshall's marvelous opinion in *Marbury* teaches us to reject this false dichotomy.[21] His argument for judicial review is based on the essential features of America's written Constitution that are rooted in unwritten understandings, which are necessary to faithfully interpret the constitutional text. The same, however, is true of Judge Gibson's argument, which rejected judicial review.

Still, Kavanaugh is right to call our attention to the text; it informs us about the structure and logic of the Constitution, as well as articulating constitutional values, standards, and principles. But it alone does not do the labor textualists assign to it. We can be committed to faithfully following the text of the Constitution and still need to move beyond the precise words of the Constitution to faithfully interpret it. As the Yale law professor Akhil Amar reminds us, there's a distinction between reading the Constitution "literally" and reading the Constitution "faithfully."[22] Nearly all contemporary jurists think that *Marbury* is rightly decided, even while agreeing that judicial review is *not* specified by the constitutional text but inferred (constructed?) from the political theory implicit in the Constitution. When we consider just how Marshall turns to the text in *Marbury*, we could do the same with *nearly any clause of the Constitution*. Marshall asks: If the

Constitution commands that no state shall pass an ex post facto law and a state does so, doesn't this violate the very idea of the written Constitution as fundamental law?

If the Fourteenth Amendment declares that no state shall deny any person within its jurisdiction the equal protection of the law and a state does so, doesn't this violate the Constitution? Yes! The hard labor here necessarily turns on the underlying constitutional logic that makes sense of the precise text of the Constitution. How do we determine whether a specific law violates a constitutional provision? When same-sex couples objected to state laws that prohibited them from marrying one another precisely because they were of the same sex, they were making a claim about the due process and the equal protection clauses of the Fourteenth Amendment. Their claim was not about the best policy or about doing justice *outside* the Constitution. It was about a *constitutional* command: No state shall deny any person liberty without due process of law or deny any person in its jurisdiction the equal protection of the laws.

Now it may be that these couples were wrong, as Justice Scalia argued in his dissenting opinion in *Obergefell v. Hodges* (2015). But Scalia, just as much as the same-sex couple making the claim, offered an underlying theory of the Constitution that said the best interpretation of the equal protection clause and the due process clause does not extend them to same-sex marriage. The couple pressing the claim offered a different theory to make sense of the text. Both of these claims turn to "a written document to which all may have recourse" in making their arguments.[23] On their face, both claims turn to constitutional text and are compatible with it. The text does not tell us which interpretation is better; it is our unwritten theory that does that. Yet again, the real debate here is a debate about the best understanding of unwritten principles.

The (Un)Written Constitution is not hostile to textualism or originalism. Originalism comes, as we will see, in a wide variety of forms and traces its lineage to Madison.[24] I do not do justice to the sophistication and subtlety of the various strands of originalist scholarship; that's not the aim of this book.[25] Though when I do take it up, you're likely to notice a profound disconnect between originalism as defended and practiced by its political supporters and by judges, and originalism as a wide-ranging set of academic constitutional theories. But this book does not defend a particular theory of constitutional interpretation; it does not put forward a correct mode or approach to constitutional interpretation. It seeks to illustrate that *all* approaches to constitutional interpretation rest on unwritten ideas. All approaches rest on some sort of political theory of the Constitution that frames how we should understand constitutional text.[26] Many of our most important constitutional disputes, contrary to some of our most prominent textualist jurists, are not about whether to follow the text; they are disputes about what fidelity to text requires. They are disputes about our unwritten understandings, ideas, commitments, and principles. This is an inescapable feature of our written Constitution, not a defect or a bug. What approach is most faithful to the Constitution? What approach best captures the meaning of constitutional text? I leave that judgment to the reader. But given the nature of the written Constitution, we should doubt that any single approach or theory is going to settle our constitutional debates. Indeed, as the Stanford University constitutional historian Jack N. Rakove reminds us, our efforts to interpret the Constitution frequently require that we interpret historical *debates* about the Constitution. We should not forget that it is often a "debate [we] are interpreting."[27]

If textualist and originalist jurists have been reluctant to note the inevitability of going beyond the text, defenders of the "unwritten constitution" have been too indulgent about doing so. Thomas Grey, a Stanford law professor and leading defender of the unwritten Constitution, has gone so far as to argue that courts should accept an *additional* role beyond interpretation as "the expounder of basic national ideals of individual liberty and fair treatment, even when the content of these ideals is not expressed as a matter of positive law in the written Constitution."[28] Asking whether judges should "enforce principles of liberty and justice when the normative content of those principles is not to be found within the four corners of our founding document" makes it sound as if judges are turning "outside" of the Constitution to free-floating moral and philosophical principles that cannot be justified by constitutional text.[29] Such a defense of the unwritten Constitution invites the criticisms textualists and originalists have leveled at it. Grey made things worse by distinguishing between

"interpretivism" and "non-interpretivism" in constitutional adjudication: as if some were trying to "interpret" the Constitution while
others had moved beyond it. Compounding the problem, textualists
and originalists were dubbed "interpretivists," while those expounding
the unwritten constitution were dubbed "non-interpretivists." Happily,
Grey long ago rejected his initial framing, casting his defense of the unwritten Constitution as "interpretivist." And scholarly debate long ago
moved on from this distinction.[30]

Yet, as we've seen, this distinction remains powerful in popular and
judicial constitutional discourse.[31] Think of originalist jurists on the
Court who frequently invoke this distinction or of senators who insist
they will only vote to confirm judges who are "strict constructionists"
(a phrase rejected by most originalists). Justice Scalia looms large
in this public discourse. Even before his death, he was offered up by
conservatives as the model jurist—the great *textualist*—who relished
exposing departures from text as departures from the Constitution.[32]
The (Un)Written Constitution corrects this framing. The American
Constitution necessarily depends on unwritten concepts and
understandings because of its brevity; it is fewer than 8,000 words (including amendments). As Chief Justice John Marshall famously put it:

A Constitution, to contain an accurate detail of all the subdivisions
of which its great powers will admit, and of all the means by which
they may be carried into execution, would partake of the prolixity
of a legal code, and could scarcely be embraced by the human mind.
It would probably never be understood by the public. Its nature,
therefore, requires that only its great outlines should be marked, its
important objects designated, and the minor ingredients which compose those objects be deduced from the nature of the objects themselves. That this idea was entertained by the framers of the American
Constitution is not only to be inferred from the nature of the instrument, but from the language.[33]

Drawing from judicial opinions and political practices rather than
scholarly disquisition, I focus largely on Supreme Court opinions
and the arguments of the justices to make visible the unwritten
understandings and ideas that drive textual interpretation. Beyond

Supreme Court opinions, I turn to prominent political figures such as James Madison, who had a hand in working out constitutional meaning based on sparse text. In explicating the Constitution, these judicial and political opinions offer us a great debate on the political theory that underlies the written Constitution.[34] Across a range of constitutional disputes—from the separation of powers to the meaning of freedom of speech, from partisan gerrymandering to the reach and limits of Congress's power to regulate interstate commerce, from racial discrimination to same-sex marriage—*The (Un)Written Constitution* illuminates the unwritten understandings that inform our disputes about the written Constitution. Whether originalist or not, nearly everyone agrees that the ideas of those who framed the Constitution and its amendments should help shape our interpretation of text. So, too, with those who ratified the Constitution and its amendments. But just how determinative should these understandings be? Are we bound by historical expectations? Or are we only bound by the general sentiments and aspirations of those who framed and ratified the Constitution?[35] Does this include the political theory that informed American constitutional institutions and ideas? Does it include philosophical and moral principles—what Edward Corwin, a prominent constitutional thinker at Princeton University, famously called the higher law background of American constitutional law—that inform and underlie the Constitution?[36] To what degree should tradition, precedent, and prudential considerations inform our interpretation of text? We won't find the answers to these questions in constitutional text. Yet we cannot escape these questions. They lurk behind our debates on how to best understand the Constitution, and they largely turn on unwritten ideas.

At the heart of this work is a two-step analysis. The first step brings out the unwritten understandings, concepts, and principles that all approaches to constitutional interpretation rest on. Once this is made visible, the second step illustrates that our most foundational constitutional debates are best understood as debates between different unwritten understandings, concepts, and principles. These debates about unwritten ideas are debates about how to make the best sense of the written Constitution. This point is particularly important because the public face of textualism and originalism—unlike the scholarly analysis—obscures this truth.[37] Yet the fact that all constitutional interpretation rests on unwritten ideas about the political theory that underlies the Constitution does not make it illegitimate interpretation, nor does it mean that anything goes. It means, rather, that we have the burden of explaining the unwritten understandings we draw on to make the best sense of the written Constitution. We cannot escape making constitutional judgments that are *not* based in text. Such judgments, like Scalia's defense of originalism, are *constructed* by constitutional interpreters as part of an effort to apply constitutional text. There is no getting around this. There is no safe space that allows us to avoid constitutional judgments that are not determined by text, just the reasons we give for making them. Whether we want to think of them as implicit in text, within the Constitution itself, part of America's small "c" constitution, or as essential background principles and concepts are all ideas we will consider throughout this book.

Chapters 1 and 2 focus on the two most influential textualists on the Supreme Court in the modern era—Justices Black and Scalia—to highlight their own unwritten assumptions as instrumental to their reading of text, as well as to demonstrate that these unwritten understandings drove their antagonisms with their critics on and off the bench.

Chapter 1 takes up textualism's most famous expositor from the Supreme Court, Justice Hugo Black. Appointed by President Franklin Delano Roosevelt in the mid-1930s, Justice Black called himself a "constitutional literalist" and was famous for carrying a pocket Constitution with him long before Justice Kavanaugh did. Pointing to the text of the Bill of Rights, Black is best known for his insistence that the Fourteenth Amendment applies all of the rights enumerated there to the states (the doctrine known as incorporation). Perhaps even more importantly, Justice Black crusaded against the notion of unenumerated constitutional rights: If a right was not *specifically and clearly enumerated* in constitutional text, then it was *not a constitutional right*. Black's lucid and parsimonious jurisprudence is seductive, but it is not nearly as obvious as it appears at first glance. Many of Black's most important judgments rest on unwritten assumptions that are not neatly derived from text. Not only was he too prone to cast those he disagreed with as engaging in "natural law" reasoning, but we also have been too apt to read Black's judicial antagonists through his distorted lens. A Warren Court liberal and New Dealer, Justice Black was nonetheless a key figure in the return of originalism as central to understanding constitutional text.

Chapter 2 looks at originalism and textualism with a particular focus on Justice Antonin Scalia, appointed by President Ronald Reagan. Scalia is originalism's most visible advocate—evident in his being taken as the model jurist for conservatives and Republicans, including three sitting Supreme Court justices—even if originalism as a theory of interpretation has run far beyond Justice Scalia. While Scalia merges textualism and originalism, his jurisprudence reveals that they do not always go together. Originalism, in his hands, can limit and confine constitutional text, particularly as he relies heavily on history and tradition. Yet how and when history and tradition should control our understanding of text turns on Scalia's desire to limit judicial discretion. Similarly, Scalia's jurisprudence of original meaning, much like Justice Black's textual jurisprudence, is rooted in unwritten understandings about democracy and the nature of the judiciary that are not obviously drawn from text. While Scalia frequently chastised his colleagues for departing from the Constitution, his quarrels with them were largely over unwritten understandings and ideas.

Having made visible the unwritten understandings of the Court's two most famous textualists that drove their jurisprudential fights, chapter 3 returns to two founding-era debates. These two early conflicts reveal that sparse text can point to deeper unwritten principles and concepts at the very heart of America's constitutional republic. The first debate deals with the prohibition on religious tests for office in Article VI. While the text seems clear on its face—no religious tests for public office—did it apply only to Protestant sects? Only to Christians? Or did it mean that even Jews and Muslims could hold office? James Iredell, later a Supreme Court justice, drew out the text's underlying principles of religious liberty and toleration to explain that the text must be understood in general terms, extending the logic of religious liberty to all, years before the First Amendment was ratified.

In a similar fashion, James Madison drew out the logic of republican government to explain the text of the First Amendment regarding freedom of speech and press after the government passed the Sedition Act of 1798. Many legal thinkers at the time thought the text— "Congress shall make no law abridging the freedom of speech or the press"—was perfectly consistent with the British common law doctrine of "no prior restraint" (while the government could not restrain speech prior to publication, it could punish if after the fact). Madison rejected this understanding as fundamentally at odds with the unwritten principles of the new Constitution. Madison and his antagonists agreed on the wording of constitutional text; they disagreed profoundly on the principles and political theory that underlie it.

Chapter 4 turns to the separation of powers. Textualists point to the first three articles of the Constitution, which make up the bulk of the Constitution's seven articles. These articles outline and allocate power between the branches of government, as well as establish checks and balances among them. Yet many questions remain—basic questions such as the nature of "the executive power." The chapter first turns to debates about executive power with regard to the president's ability to remove officers within the executive branch, and how executive power is constructed in relation to legislative and judicial power based on unwritten ideas. The chapter then turns to the allocation of constitutional power regarding issues of war and peace within the separation of powers to illustrate that disputes about the war power, just like disputes about "the executive power," turn on unwritten ideas. These debates have been with us since the founding, with remarkably little disagreement about constitutional text but profound disagreement on the unwritten concepts that underlie it.

Chapter 5 returns to the unwritten ideas that underlie all approaches to constitutional interpretation. If the text of the Constitution remains unchanged but our unwritten understandings change, does that change the Constitution? Can the constitution be both fixed and perpetually changing? The text of the equal protection clause of the Fourteenth Amendment has been the same since it was ratified in 1868. For most of that time, it was perfectly acceptable for states to prohibit women from entering certain occupations—being a lawyer or a bartender, for example. That's changed. Was it legitimate? Some jurists and scholars think that constitutional interpretation should include applying general principles and understandings in ways we may never have thought about before. Others insist that such work should come by way of democratic legislation or constitutional amendment, not by way of constitutional interpretation by unelected judges. Each approach rests on unwritten understandings—on a political theory that underlies the Constitution, which is the source of our debates about how to faithfully follow the written Constitution.

Any approach to constitutional interpretation must balance and weigh the different parts of the Constitution. Even if we agree that we are bound by the formal written Constitution, what that entails cannot be answered by constitutional text alone. How we balance different constitutional rules, commands, and concepts will largely be determined by our unwritten ideas. When it comes to our deepest constitutional debates, we cannot just read the words of the Constitution.

Yet I conclude by urging us to begin with these words. Not just judges and justices, but all public officials. By way of Article VI, every public official takes an oath to support the Constitution before taking office. They should know what this entails. But reading the text will only highlight its inadequacy. Alone the text does not answer many of the constitutional questions we are required to wrestle with. So where do we turn? We cannot escape this question. Wherever we turn to illuminate constitutional text, we are implicitly or explicitly rendering constitutional judgments. Giving our reasons for doing so is the burden—and the promise—of constitutional self-government.

1

Text and Textualism

In the beginning was the word, and the word was with
God, and the word was God.

—John 1:1

Justice Hugo Black was famous for extolling the text of the
Constitution. Much like the textually based strand of Protestantism
he was raised on, Black took the words of the Constitution as akin to
American scripture. Not only did he advocate a constitutional faith, he
also called himself a "constitutional literalist" because of his insistence
on the plain meaning of constitutional text. Black reasoned that any
movement beyond the words of the Constitution itself was to indulge
opinions based on "natural" rights and justice. Such an enterprise was
no longer constitutional interpretation, but an act of constitutional
apostasy. Black was known for pulling out his pocket Constitution and
asking just where in the written Constitution, say, the right to privacy
could be found.

As a jurist, Black was an eloquent and passionate advocate of textually enumerated rights, as well as a powerful critic of the idea that it
was the duty of the Court to keep the Constitution "in tune with the
times." Black, a sitting senator from Alabama, was Franklin Delano
Roosevelt's (FDR) first appointment to the Supreme Court, where he
served from 1937–1971. If critical of the notion of a living constitution that FDR often extoled, Justice Black shared his sense that during
the early years of the New Deal, the Supreme Court was imposing its
values on the Constitution in order to overturn popular and democratically enacted legislation. Skepticism of judicial activism and
overreach shaped Black's understanding of the written Constitution.
Constitutional text was a limitation on such judicial activism.

The (Un)Written Constitution. George Thomas, Oxford University Press. © Oxford University Press 2021.
DOI: 10.1093/oso/9780197555972.003.0002

The Logic of Enumerated Rights

Justice Black argued that the judiciary was on solid constitutional ground when it was enforcing the "particular standards enumerated in the Bill of Rights and other parts of the Constitution."[1] And this was because, for Black, the "people wanted and demanded a Bill of Rights written into their Constitution."[2] The act of textually enumerating rights in a bill of rights is what marked them off for *judicial protection*. The ratification of the Fourteenth Amendment then applied the rights enumerated in the Bill of Rights to the states by way of the privileges or immunities clause and the due process clause. The Fourteenth Amendment commands: "no State shall make or enforce any law which shall abridge the privileges or immunities of citizens of the United States; nor shall any State deprive any person of life, liberty, or property, without due process of law." Beginning with the text, you might ask what are the "privileges or immunities" of US citizenship? What "liberties" can you not be deprived of without due process of law?

Black had a ready and elegant answer: those rights enumerated in the Bill of Rights. These were the "privileges or immunities of citizenship" secured by constitutional text; the "liberty" constitutional text marked off from the democratic process.

Black first articulated his textualist position in *Adamson v. California* (1947). At the time, California allowed prosecuting attorneys in criminal trials to comment on the fact that defendants did not take the stand to testify. The state could thus insinuate that the defendant was guilty if they declined to testify at their trial. The Fifth Amendment, however, holds that no person "shall be compelled in any criminal case to be a witness against himself." But did the Fifth Amendment apply to the states? The Court held that it did not. In an opinion by Justice Stanley Reed, also appointed by FDR, the Court argued that only those rights "implicit in the concept of ordered liberty" were protected against the states by the Fourteenth Amendment. The Court rejected the idea that the Fourteenth Amendment incorporated the Bill of Rights against the states because not all the rights in it were central to the concept of ordered liberty.

Black took issue with the Court's nebulous standard of "ordered liberty." As Black argued in dissent, the Court's interpretation endows it "with boundless power under 'natural law' periodically to expand and contract constitutional standards to conform with the Court's conception of what, at a particular time, constitutes 'civilized decency' and 'fundamental liberty and justice.'"[3] For Black, resorting to fuzzy concepts like ordered liberty was an invitation for justices to indulge subjective preferences and engage in judicial lawmaking. Worse, the Court might then expand and contract rights—that is, what's included in ordered liberty—based on its whims.

Black further argued that his "study of the historical events that culminated in the Fourteenth Amendment" persuaded him that one of its chief objects was "to make the Bill of Rights applicable to the states."[4] Black insisted that the Court should follow "the original purpose of the Fourteenth Amendment—to extend to all the people of the nation the complete protection of the Bill of Rights." To do otherwise, was to allow the Court to determine "what, if any, provisions of the Bill of Rights will be enforced, and if so, to what degree," which would "frustrate the great design of a written Constitution."[5] Black attached an appendix to his *Adamson* dissent, which drew on historical materials to document his case. The debates over the framing of the Fourteenth Amendment illustrated, according to Black, that the privileges or immunities of citizenship referred to the rights enumerated in the Bill of Rights. The framers of the amendment sought to protect these rights against the states, which based on a Supreme Court decision from the 1830s did not apply to the states.[6] The Fourteenth Amendment now secured these rights for all Americans regardless of what state they resided in. The historical accuracy of Black's analysis remains the subject of debate.[7] Yet, in turning to historical materials to discern the original intent of those who framed the Fourteenth Amendment in interpreting constitutional text, Black made an important contribution to the modern development of originalist jurisprudence.

Black's fear that abstract constitutional clauses invited the Court to read its moral and political inclinations into the Constitution also had a marked influence on the development of originalism. And the Court's own language lent credence to Black's worries. A few years after *Adamson*, in *Rochin v. California* (1952), the Fifth Amendment's prohibition on self-incrimination was once again before the Court. Three police officers entered Rochin's home, suspecting him of dealing drugs.

When asked about two capsules on his bedside table, Rochin quickly put them in his mouth. A struggle with the police ensued as they attempted to extract the pills from Rochin's mouth. Failing, the police seized Rochin against his will and took him to the hospital where doctors, again against Rochin's objections, were ordered to pump his stomach. He vomited morphine pills.

This was too much for the Court. In a unanimous opinion, Justice Felix Frankfurter, a former Harvard Law professor and another FDR appointee, insisted that the methods used here "are too close to the rack and the screw" and that this is "conduct that shocks the conscience."[8] Yet Justice Frankfurter did not find that this conduct violated the Fifth Amendment's clause against self-incrimination. Rather, he argued that it violated general notions of due process as understood by the history of "English-speaking peoples." The standards of justice and due process that prohibited such conduct were so "rooted in the traditions and conscience of our people as to be ranked as fundamental or are implicit in the concept of ordered liberty."[9] Frankfurter understood the text—due process of law—as part of an historical conception rooted in Anglo-American jurisprudence. Judges were tasked in this scheme with discerning due process, which itself was an evolving standard. Frankfurter insisted that this flexible understanding of due process was rooted in history and tradition and not based on the mere subjective preferences of the justices. Indeed, Frankfurter disavowed that the standards the justices were drawing on were their own or the revival of natural law. Standards of due process evolved as a part of meaning and tradition under the Constitution. Yet Frankfurter did acknowledge that in due process cases, as well as many others, the Constitution places on the Court the responsibility of judgment. There is no escaping this—even by way of constitutional text: "Words being symbols do not speak without a gloss." This was true even of "more specific provisions." Black was not persuaded.

Limiting Judicial Will

Justice Black thought expansive and vague concepts, such as due process, could be tamed by constitutional text. Black's worry that the

Court was going beyond the Constitution was a continuous refrain. Understanding due process by way of "ordered liberty," he argued, "vested this Court with . . . unlimited power to invalidate laws" based on subjective considerations of natural justice, or this "natural law formula" left an "incongruous excrescence on our Constitution."[10] This entire mode of constitutional interpretation was "itself a violation of our Constitution." Black saw this as overturning the proper relationship between those who make the law and those who interpret it: "it subtly conveys to courts, at the expense of legislatures, ultimate power over public policies in fields where no specific provision of the Constitution limits legislative power."[11] The solution, for Black, was found in constitutional text. Fourteenth Amendment due process should be understood as nothing more, nor nothing less, than incorporating the Bill of Rights against the states. Not only was this consistent with original intent, but it would also limit and bind judicial interpretation.

In *Griswold v. Connecticut* (1965) Black developed the full logic of his textualism. Griswold dealt with a Connecticut statute passed in the late nineteenth century that prohibited the dissemination and use of contraceptives—even among married couples. The Court found that the Constitution protected a sphere of privacy that allowed married couples to make choices about birth control and family planning independently of state regulation. The Court split on its reasoning, situating such a right within the "penumbras" of the Bill of Rights; as part of fundamental principles of liberty protected by the Ninth Amendment and the Fourteenth Amendment; and simply as part of Fourteenth Amendment due process on its own terms. Justice Black's vehement dissent asserted that there was simply no ground on which the Court might rest such a constitutional judgment. Try as you might, this right was not in the Constitution: the "Court talks about a constitutional 'right to privacy' as though there is some constitutional provision or provisions forbidding any law ever to be passed which might abridge the 'privacy' of individuals. But there is not." Even if specific textual provisions, such as the Fourth Amendment's prohibition of unreasonable searches and seizures, might protect a limited form of privacy, we could not deduce from that a more general right to privacy that included the right of married couples to use contraception. The Court, Black argued, should stick to the simple language of the Constitution: "I like my privacy as well as the next one, but I am compelled to admit that government has a right to invade it unless prohibited by some specific constitutional provision."[12]

Black's argument for incorporation should by now be obvious: if the right is not enumerated in the Bill of Rights, it is not constitutionally protected. Black's *Griswold* dissent, however, is of particular interest because he also took on the argument from the Ninth Amendment. The text of the amendment, recall, commands "the enumeration in the Constitution, of certain rights, shall not be construed to deny or disparage others retained by the people." Yet Black insisted that the Ninth Amendment cannot be read as empowering the judiciary to articulate and protect unwritten rights against legislative judgments. The crux, for Black, is there is simply no way for the judiciary to determine what rights count under the Ninth Amendment. This very effort was based on subjective judgments. Therefore, the Ninth Amendment had to be read as a reminder to the people that the powers of the national government were limited. But this is a rule for the people, not for the Court. And if the people wanted to change the Constitution, they had recourse by way of constitutional amendment.

Text and Constitutional Change

Black argued that the text of the Constitution, by way of Article V, provided a way for the people to protect rights they thought should be added to the Constitution. If the people so chose. By way of constitutional amendment, the people can secure whatever rights they think essential. That, in fact, was what the people had done in framing and ratifying the original Bill of Rights. And it was because the people singled out these rights for protection in constitutional text by way of the first ten amendments to the Constitution that the Court was empowered to enforce them against acts of the legislature. By way of text, these rights had been singled out and marked off against legislative encroachment. Until the text of the Constitution was amended by an act of the people to protect a general right of privacy, the judiciary had no business protecting such rights based on unwritten assumptions. This was just as true of the Fourteenth Amendment's due process clause, as we saw earlier in the chapter. To read liberties into the Fourteenth Amendment that were not textually specified in the Bill of Rights, was to draw on "mysterious and uncertain natural law concepts" relying on "subjective considerations of 'natural justice.'"[13]

Black's arguments pointed to a written Constitution created and ratified by the people that would become a hallmark of originalism. In doing so, the people marked off certain rights for protection against future democratic majorities. Where rights are textually specified, the Court is empowered by the written Constitution to protect them against the legislature. And the people remain free, by way of constitutional amendment, to alter the written Constitution. But the written Constitution is to be maintained as written until such an act of amendment. Enforcing the terms of the written Constitution is to enforce democratic norms: the Constitution is an act of the people that binds us.

Text and Justice Black's Unwritten Understandings

We should notice that part of Black's argument, while insisting on the centrality of text, rests on his understanding of the proper role of the legislature and judiciary in a democracy. In Black's understanding of democracy, the legislature is given wide sweep, while the judiciary is narrowly confined. By and large, Black does not insist that legislatures must point to constitutional text to justify their exercise of power: legislative action is presumed constitutional and sanctified, so to speak, because it represents the people. The judiciary should not be in a position to second-guess the legislature—unless the Constitution very clearly and carefully marked off specific textual provisions that authorized judicial protection. In the vast majority of cases, the democratic process should simply get its way. Black's understanding of the legislature and judiciary—that informs his take on the written Constitution—is not shared by all. Even Justice Frankfurter, who in general had a robust sense of judicial deference to the legislature, thought that the judiciary was positioned to expound concepts like due process of law because of its independence and unique learning in the law. Frankfurter thought Black misunderstood the role of courts in our democracy. What if the judiciary is positioned in the constitutional scheme precisely to keep the legislative branch in check? As an earlier Court put it, "It is a question of which of two powers or rights shall prevail—the power of the State to legislate or the right of the individual to liberty of person and freedom of contract?"[14] In the (in)famous case of *Lochner v. New York* from 1905, the Court struck down a maximum-hours law for bakers. Whether you think the opinion was rightly decided then or now, the crucial point is that this mode of constitutional reasoning runs far beyond liberty of contract; it positions the judiciary as policing the boundaries of legislative power. While the legislature has wide sweep to pass laws regulating the health, welfare, and safety of the people, what if, under the guise of exercising its legitimate power, it acted in impermissible ways? This is essentially John Marshall's question from *Marbury*. Should the judiciary be aggressive in policing the boundaries of legislative power? Should it be deferential to majoritarian democracy? Should it only exercise such power in a self-evidently clear case? The text does not answer these questions for us.

Black loathed the logic of the *Lochner* Court (from the early years of the twentieth century) and frequently referred to the opinion. It was the very epitome of "substantive due process" with its subjective considerations of "natural justice," finding laws unconstitutional because they were "arbitrary." In fairness to the *Lochner* Court, it said not a word about natural law or natural justice but rooted its arguments in liberty under the Fourteenth Amendment; it also recognized the state's power to limit liberty in all sorts of ways *if* the state's regulation was aimed at a *legitimate* purpose—like requiring vaccinations against an outbreak of smallpox for the public health.[15] But was a law that limited the hours bakers could work legitimately aimed at health and safety? Was baking different from other professions, which were not limited in such ways? Probably. But the argument before the Court actually focused on the health *of the consumer* and not the *health of the baker*.[16]

Consider other cases. What about a Nebraska law that prohibited the teaching of foreign languages in elementary school? An Oregon law that prohibited private secondary education? A Washington law that prescribed a minimum wage for women but not men? These laws were struck down as arbitrary violations of due process because the regulation at issue was not tethered to a legitimate health, welfare, or safety concern. In these cases, the Court did not simply take the legislature at its word: it often teased out arbitrary distinctions. In the Nebraska case, the prohibition on teaching a foreign language forbid a student from either learning German or having a subject taught in German. Yet it allowed Latin, Greek, and Hebrew. The goal was to "promote civic development," and Nebraska sought to do so by prohibiting the teaching of German, French, Spanish, and Italian.[17] But were the languages harmful in and of themselves? Why the exception for other languages? The Court recognized the state interest in promoting civic education but found the law here limited a fundamental right to learn free from arbitrary coercion. No doubt, this gives the judiciary quite a bit of leeway in policing the boundaries of legislative power. Yet defenders of this understanding argue that the written Constitution itself embraces this understanding: it provides for the protection of individual liberty against overbearing democratic majorities.[18] This is precisely the task the written Constitution assigns judges. And the written Constitution itself protects "liberty" as a general concept.

In contrast, when Black encounters these more open-ended constitutional provisions, like "liberty" in the Fourteenth Amendment's due process clause, he argues that we must read "liberty" as only protecting rights enumerated elsewhere—that is, as mentioned, in the Bill of Rights. To do otherwise is to invite judicial lawmaking. We must interpret text in a manner that cabins and confines judicial lawmaking. Yet this value is not derived from constitutional text. Black justifies this based on his conception of the role of judges and on the importance of limiting judicial discretion in interpreting constitutional text. Advising an Israeli inquiring about whether to write a constitution or not, Justice Black insisted: make "a constitution immediately, and make it so stringent that no Supreme Court can evade it."[19] Black thought a written constitution could tie our hands—especially the hands of judges—in ways that would limit, even eliminate, our discretion. He frequently quoted Thomas Jefferson's adage that "our peculiar security is in the possession of a written Constitution. Let us not make it a blank paper by construction."[20]

But Black's judgments rest on understandings rooted in his view of democracy. This is as true of Justice Black as it is of defenders of *Lochner*-style constitutional reasoning. In fact, defenders of *Lochner*-style reasoning agree with Jefferson's idea of a written Constitution. They worry, indeed, that Black's approach to text essentially gives *all power* to legislatures unless individuals can trump that power with a specific constitutional right.[21] This is an argument about what understanding of democracy underlies the written Constitution, not an argument where one side embraces the written Constitution and the other side abandons it in favor of natural justice.

Why should we understand text as Black does? Black's insistence on confining liberty to textually specified rights derived from the Bill of Rights stems from his desire to cabin judicial discretion by tethering it to clear textual commands. Black reads constitutional text through the lens of limiting judicial discretion in a majoritarian democracy. He does acknowledge that text on occasion invites judicial discretion. The Fourth Amendment's prohibition against "unreasonable" searches and seizures calls on the judiciary to determine what is "unreasonable." But this is different, he argues, than determining what is a "reasonable" regulation of liberty under the Fourteenth Amendment's due process clause.

Justice Frankfurter, Black's great antagonist and interlocutor, argued that the "Due Process Clauses places upon this Court the duty of exercising judgment" that cannot be captured by text alone but depends on an understanding of the judicial role in the constitutional scheme. Against Black, Frankfurter insisted that to "believe that this judicial exercise of judgment could be avoided by freezing 'due process of law' at some fixed stage of time or thought is to suggest that the most important aspects of constitutional adjudication is a function for inanimate machines and not for judges, for whom the independence safeguarded by Article III of the Constitution was designed and who are presumably guided by established standards of judicial behavior."[22]

Frankfurter tried to persuade Black that discretion and independent judgment were inescapable features of judging. A judiciary engaged in constitutional interpretation cannot escape making such judgments. Justice John Marshall Harlan II, concurring in the Connecticut contraception case, went even further and explicitly took on Black's argument: "the thesis that by limiting the content of the Due Process Clause of the Fourteenth Amendment to the protection of rights which can be found elsewhere in the Constitution, in this instance in the Bill of Rights, judges will thus be confined to 'interpretation' of specific constitutional provisions, and will thereby be restrained from introducing their own notions of constitutional right and wrong into the 'vague contours of the Due Process Clause' is more hollow than real."[23]

Like the debate about the proper balance between the legislature and the judiciary within American constitutional democracy, this is a profound dispute about the nature of the judiciary in the constitutional scheme. Black's arguments are powerful. But his argument about the judicial role does not depend on text. Article III of the Constitution, which creates the Supreme Court and establishes its independence, does not answer this debate. Frankfurter and Harlan are operating from the same textual ground that Black is. This is true, if less obviously, when we turn to the due process clause as well.

Incorporation as Textual?

Here again is the Fourteenth Amendment command at issue: "nor shall any State deprive any person of life, liberty, or property, without due process of law." Black argues that liberty in this text should be understood as shorthand for the rights listed in the Bill of Rights. This is the "liberty" the Fourteenth Amendment protects by way of due process. To protect anything less for Black is to distort these textual provisions. To protect anything more is to go beyond what the Constitution actually protects. In *Griswold*, Justice Harlan disputes Black's reading: the Fourteenth Amendment's due process clause, he avers, "stands . . . on its own bottom."[24]

No less than Black, Harlan insists on the text of the Constitution. And contrary to Justice Black, the text itself does not say anything about incorporation. It says "liberty." Why should we read that as shorthand for the Bill of Rights? If that is what the framers of the Fourteenth Amendment wanted to say they could have said it. They could have used that precise language in text. One could easily imagine the Fourteenth Amendment stating, "no state shall deprive any person of the liberties enumerated in the Bill of Rights." Or "rights listed in the Bill of Rights apply to the states." Or, even more precisely, given Black's argument: "no state shall deny any citizen of a right enumerated in the first eight amendments to the Constitution." But that is not the language of the text. As Black himself says, "One of the most effective ways of diluting or expanding a constitutionally guaranteed right is to substitute for the crucial word or words of a constitutional guarantee another word or words, more or less flexible and more or less restricted in meaning."[25] Yet, is this just what Black does in arguing for incorporation and only incorporation?

This may well be the best interpretation of the text, but it depends on judgments about democracy and the role of the court, not on text. To reach his conclusions, Black turns briefly to the history of the framing of the Fourteenth Amendment and more generally to limiting judicial discretion. Perhaps he is right. Black's appendix to his *Adamson* dissent, turning to congressional debates over the Fourteenth Amendment, was a turn to discover original intent. Jurists and scholars still debate what rights are included within the "privileges or immunities" of citizens and what "liberty" is protected by due process on originalist grounds. Yet it is interesting to note that when Black wrote, the consensus was strongly against his interpretation, even if the scholarly consensus became much more favorable to his argument, if not his history, in subsequent years.[26]

The Ninth Amendment and the Logic of a Written Constitution

Black's putative textualism faces additional textual burdens. Most evidently, the Ninth Amendment's command that the "enumeration in the Constitution, of certain rights, shall not be construed to deny or disparage others retained by the people." As Black argues, the general character of this amendment emphasizes the limits on the federal government; it should not be understood as an open-ended invitation for judges to read unenumerated rights into the Constitution. But if the amendment clearly refers to rights that are *not enumerated* and *should not be denied*, would this amount to reading rights "into" the Constitution or are such rights already in the Constitution? And are they in the Constitution by virtue of constitutional text?

Black's question—how do we determine these rights?—is an excellent one. At the same time, even if the best interpretation of the Ninth Amendment does not invite the judicial protection of rights, it does seem to be a perhaps non-enforceable constitutional command to *not* interpret the text of the Constitution as Justice Black does. Black, after all, insists that only enumerated rights are secured by the Constitution. The Ninth Amendment, even if it is only there as a guide for interpretation, commands otherwise. One reading of the Ninth Amendment is that it places the burden on the government—demanding that the government justify its exercise of power when it legislates.[27] Notice that almost all the textual commands that protect rights do so by limiting governmental power rather than specifically granting rights. The First Amendment commands, "Congress shall make no law." The Fourteenth Amendment commands that "no state shall." Much as the Ninth commands us that we "shall not" construe the Constitution in a certain way—that is, the way that Justice Black does. As Black argues, the "government has a right to invade [privacy] unless prohibited by some specific constitutional provision."[28] Historically speaking, the Ninth Amendment has its roots in concerns that a bill of rights might (wrongly) lead us to interpret the Constitution just as Black does—assuming that unless an individual can point to a specifically enumerated right in the Constitution, the government has the power to prohibit that right.

At the core of this jurisprudential dispute, which has been with us since the ratification debates over the Constitution, is how we understand constitutional democracy. In Federalist 84, Alexander Hamilton argued against a bill of rights. He insisted that bills of rights were things carved out for the people against a powerful government. They were, in essence, concessions from the monarch to the people bestowed by the government. But in a limited and written constitution created by the people, it was the people who gave the government a limited grant of power by way of enumerating power.[29] Rights should remain unenumerated precisely because they are *retained by the people*. James Wilson, a leading participant at the Constitutional

Convention and one of the original justices appointed to the Supreme Court by President George Washington, pushed this argument at the Pennsylvania Ratifying Convention where he insisted that a bill of rights would corrupt the logic of a written constitution rooted in popular sovereignty. A bill of rights risked reversing the logic of constitutional government by assuming that the government has the power to do something unless an individual can point to an enumerated right that prohibits the government from doing so. The logic of our written Constitution, however, should place the burden on the government to justify its use of power by pointing to textual provisions that allow it to act.[30]

However powerful these arguments were, securing ratification of the Constitution depended on creating a bill or rights. James Madison, who began as a skeptic, was ultimately persuaded to concede the necessity of a bill of rights as part of securing the Constitution's ratification in Virginia. As Madison wrote to his good friend Thomas Jefferson, a strong advocate of a bill of rights, he thought that a bill of rights might be most useful in shaping the public mind: teaching citizens about their rights and about the logic of constitutional government.[31] The written text was educative in this regard. This was particularly true when it came to the Ninth and Tenth Amendments. The Ninth, in particular, was meant to acknowledge the power of Hamilton's and Wilson's arguments against a bill of rights, recognizing that not all rights retained by the people could be easily enumerated. The Ninth Amendment could serve as a textual reminder of this logic.

Constitutional text itself—by way of clauses like the Ninth Amendment, the due process clause, and the privileges or immunities clause—points to unspecified rights that may be protected by way of the written Constitution. Yet Justice Black argues that any movement in this direction is to engage in natural law thinking "outside" the Constitution, corrupting the role of courts in a democracy. In his powerful dissenting opinion in *Griswold*, Black equates the protection of unenumerated rights with "natural justice." But is the equation correct?

In making this argument, Black turned to one of the first Supreme Court cases, *Calder v. Bull* (1798). Constitutional text prohibited ex post facto laws in Article I, Section 9 and Section 10 (the former aimed at the Congress, the latter aimed at the states). Black repaired to Justice

James Iredell's opinion in *Calder* because while it articulated the Court's power of judicial review it also sought to articulate limits to this power. Black thus quoted Justice Iredell, another of President Washington's first appointments to the Supreme Court, at length. Iredell first stated the obvious: if an act of Congress or of the state legislatures violated constitutional provisions it is "unquestionably" void. Iredell went on to say, however, the if the Congress or a state legislature "shall pass a law, within the scope of their constitutional power, the Court cannot pronounce it to be void, merely because it is, in their judgment, contrary to the principles of natural justice."[32]

To be sure, there are scholars and jurists who have turned to moral and natural law principles as underlying and limiting the written Constitution. The point is that Black argues that any protection of unenumerated rights must rest on the theory that justices are entitled to strike down laws that they view as against the principles of natural justice and morality whether or not the written Constitution embraces them. But that is not the argument, for example, that Black's fellow justices made in *Griswold*. As we have seen, Justice Harlan insisted the Fourteenth Amendment's due process clause rested on its own bottom, not on natural law or moral justice. He argued that the textual liberty protected under the due process clause was both wider and narrower than the rights listed in the Bill of Rights.

The question is, does constitutional text itself call for the protection of unspecified constitutional rights? Interestingly, Justice Iredell's own argument about a bill of rights at the North Carolina Ratifying Convention suggests that he saw a distinction between unenumerated constitutional rights and natural justice reasoning. It is possible to accept the former and reject the latter. As Iredell argued, if we are not careful about our logic, a bill of rights might operate as a "snare rather than as a protection." And this is because "[n]o man, let his ingenuity be what it will, could enumerate all the individual rights not relinquished by this Constitution." Clearly, Iredell believed that there were rights *not relinquished but not enumerated*. Following Black's example let me quote Iredell at length.

> Suppose, therefore, an enumeration of a great many, but an omission of some, and that, long after all traces of our present disputes were at

an end, any of the omitted rights should be invaded, and the invasion be complained of; what would be the plausible answer of the government to such a complaint? Would they not naturally say, "We live at a great distance from the time when this Constitution was established. We can judge of it much better by the ideas of it entertained at the time, than by any ideas of our own. The bill of rights, passed at that time, showed that the people did not think every power retained which was not given, else this bill of rights was not only useless, but absurd. But we are not at liberty to charge an absurdity upon our ancestors, who have given such strong proofs of their good sense, as well as their attachment to liberty. So long as the rights enumerated in the bill of rights remain unviolated, you have no reason to complain. This is not one of them."[33]

Two centuries after Iredell made this argument, this is almost precisely what Justice Black does. One could sincerely want to follow constitutional text and think that we are commanded to protect rights that are textually protected but not textually specified. We could, in fact, turn Black's accusation against him: the Court should not limit rights because we fear judicial power. Can we limit constitutional rights, textually protected constitutional rights, because we are worried that any notion of unspecified rights is the equivalent of making it up?

* * *

As Black argued in *Griswold*, it may be that the judiciary is not well suited to this task. Or maybe the risk of doing so is too high, giving far too much power to judges in a democracy. Other justices, however, have thought that so-called unenumerated rights are not nearly as elusive as Black makes them out to be. Referring to the privileges and immunities of citizenship prior to the ratification of the Fourteenth Amendment, Justice Bushrod Washington, George Washington's nephew, called these rights more tedious than difficult to enumerate.[34] Right after the passage of the Fourteenth Amendment, in the first case to consider what the privileges or immunities of citizenship were, the Court turned to Washington's opinion. In the 1873 *Slaughter-House Cases*, a divided Court saw wisdom in Washington's opinion that pointed to a host of rights that made up the privileges or immunities of citizenship. The Court disagreed whether these privileges or immunities attached to national or state citizenship. Yet neither the opinion of the Court nor the dissenting opinions thought the notion of unspecified textual rights was out of line with the recently passed amendment.[35] The debates over the framing of the amendment also point to liberties that are not included in the Bill of Rights. This is the same history that Black turned to in the appendix of his *Adamson* dissent.

This debate itself is an important one, but beyond my immediate point. I urge you to turn to the history of the Fourteenth Amendment. Turn, too, to the debates over the original Bill of Rights. These extraordinary debates engage what sort of democracy the written Constitution brought into being. My point here, however, is that at least some defenders of so-called unenumerated rights situate their arguments firmly in constitutional text. Like Black, they turn to history to make sense of the privileges and immunities of citizenship.

Justice Black also turned to substantive understandings of democracy beyond the text to frame and root his interpretation of text. In Black's case, his interpretation of text was animated by a desire to cabin and confine the problem of judicial lawmaking in what he understood to be a majoritarian democracy. In this, Justice Black had a powerful influence on Justice Antonin Scalia.

2

Text and Originalism

"The main danger in judicial interpretation of the Constitution—or, for that matter, in judicial interpretation of any law—is that the judges will mistake their own predilections for the law. Avoiding this error is the hardest part of being a conscientious judge; perhaps no conscientious judge ever succeeds entirely."[1] So, at any rate, argues Justice Antonin Scalia. And he proffers original meaning as the solution to this problem. Originalism, while not perfect—Scalia calls it "the lesser evil"—is the best method of interpretation because it "does not aggravate the principal weakness of the system, for it establishes a historical criterion that is conceptually quite separate from the preferences of the judge himself."[2] According to Scalia, original meaning is the most compelling method of constitutional interpretation because it is the only method that limits judicial discretion. Like Justice Black, Scalia's constitutional jurisprudence was driven by a desire to limit judicial discretion within a democracy.

I focus largely on Justice Scalia in thinking about textualism, originalism, and the written Constitution. Appointed to the Supreme Court by President Ronald Reagan in 1986, Justice Scalia served on the Court until his untimely death in 2016. Even after his passing, Scalia remains the most visible and influential exponent of textualism and originalism. A conservative judicial icon, Justice Scalia is the personification of textualism and originalism in the public mind.[3] Justices Neil Gorsuch, Brett Kavanaugh, and Amy Coney Barrett all consider him a mentor and role model. Barrett was even a law clerk to Scalia and has said that his judicial philosophy is her judicial philosophy. To be sure, he has his originalist critics. Randy Barnett, a law professor at Georgetown and leading originalist scholar and advocate, doubts that Scalia was an originalist at all.[4] Yale law professor Akhil Reed Amar, who also considers himself an originalist,

The (Un)Written Constitution. George Thomas, Oxford University Press. © Oxford University Press 2021.
DOI: 10.1093/oso/9780197555972.003.0003

thinks that Scalia only occasionally applied originalism and often not that well.[5] As an approach to thinking about the Constitution, originalism has gone far beyond Scalia.[6] Yet Scalia's understandings continue to shape the public mind. Not only do older originalist scholars and advocates continue to champion him, but younger defenders of originalism do so as well.[7] So, too, do politicians who want to appoint judges in the mold of Scalia, whom they often refer to as a "strict constructionist," despite the fact that he rejected the label.[8] So much so, that when Justice Scalia passed away in January of 2016, Republicans in the Senate refused to consider President Barack Obama's nomination of Judge Merrick Garland. It was the first time the Senate had done so since the 1840s! Senate Majority Leader Mitch McConnell, who denied Garland a hearing, argued that this strategy coupled with Republicans insisting on an appointee in the mold of Scalia helped deliver the election to President Donald J. Trump.[9] And for all the subtlety and sophistication of originalist scholarship, much of the public debate continues to be framed in Scalia's terms: a contest between those who stick to the text and original meaning and those who import their personal predilections into constitutional interpretation. At least Scalia's ardent defenders see it this way, in what the Columbia law professor Jamal Greene has aptly called "the selling of originalism."[10]

I want to highlight two points at the outset. First, textualism and originalism are often situated together—and for good reason—but we should note that they are not one and the same. Originalism and textualism do not always go together.[11] Second, we should note that Scalia's defense of originalism is aimed first and foremost at limiting judicial lawmaking given his understanding of democracy. His central argument for originalism is not that it leads to faithful interpretation of the text or best promotes constitutional fidelity. These loom large in Scalia's argument, but they are not his *primary* defense of originalism. And, just as originalism and textualism might be in some tension, so too might fidelity to the written Constitution and efforts to confine judicial discretion. As Scalia's former clerk, Justice Barret wrote when she was a law professor: "The Constitution's original public meaning is important not because adhering to it limits judicial discretion, but because it is the law."[12]

Text and Original Meaning

Scalia insists on interpreting the text of the Constitution as originally understood by those who ratified it. While this has strong similarities to Justice Black's textualist jurisprudence, Scalia offers a much more fully developed understanding of originalism. For starters, notice that Black emphasized the original intent of those who framed the Constitution and its amendments, while Scalia turns to the original understanding of those who ratified the Constitution and its amendments. Still, like Justice Black, he argues that text (interpreted based on original meaning) will cabin judicial discretion. Yet more fully than Black, Scalia tethered the original meaning of constitutional text to the democratic ratification of the Constitution. Black's jurisprudence pointed in this direction, but Scalia situated the ratification of the Constitution as an act of We the People as central to original meaning. The democratic act of popular sovereignty in ratifying the Constitution is what gives the Constitution its legitimacy. By enacting fundamental law by popular ratification, the sovereign people "fixed" the Constitution to govern ordinary law. It's precisely this feature that authorizes and legitimizes judicial review where courts, 200-plus years later, find contemporary laws unconstitutional.

By way of popularly ratified constitutional text, the people organized the central features of government and granted it power, which included insulating some rights from the reach of contemporary democratic majorities. Interpreting constitutional text based on original meaning not only limits judicial discretion, it also honors the democratic legitimacy of a constitution rooted in popular sovereignty. Central to this analysis, as Scalia argues, "is the perception that the Constitution, though it has an effect superior to other laws, is in its nature the sort of 'law' that is the business of the courts—an enactment that has a fixed meaning ascertainable through the usual devices familiar to those learned in the law."[13]

In the years since Scalia first championed original meaning from the bench, it has become a powerful force. It has also undergone a number of important developments, many of which have their origins in Scalia's thinking. Most importantly, the central focus is interpreting constitutional text based on the original understanding of those who ratified the text. The text is legitimate because it was ratified by an act of the sovereign people. This differs from framers' intent—or original intent—that was crucial to earlier originalist understandings, like Justice Black's. Scalia's turn to ratifiers' intent—or original meaning—has largely eclipsed the idea of framer's intent.[14]

Original meaning has been refined by subsequent scholars.[15] It is a rich and flourishing area of scholarship and debate. Yet the proliferation of terms and distinctions can be dizzying. It's not just the move from "original intent" to "original meaning," but distinctions such as "original public meaning originalism" and "original methods originalism."[16] And while once upon a time originalism was a deeply historical enterprise—focusing on historical debates about the framing and ratification or the Constitution and its amendments—it is increasingly a philosophical and linguistic debate that seeks to understand how an abstract person at the time the Constitution was ratified would have reasonably understood constitutional text.[17] For the uninitiated, it can seem strikingly abstract, somewhat reminiscent of scholastic debates about theology. I urge you to look into originalist arguments and scholarship, some of which I will touch on in this and subsequent chapters.

Despite the thriving scholarship on originalism, I focus largely on Justice Scalia's judicial opinions. He remains the most visible and important originalist—particularly as originalism is connected with textualism—in terms of his influence on constitutional law. He remains the public face of originalism: the model jurist for those who want to see textualists and originalists in the judiciary. He remains, too, the best entry point for thinking about textualism and originalism as a matter of *constitutional practice*.

Grounding Text, Grounding Judges

Let me begin with Justice Scalia's dissenting opinion in *Planned Parenthood v. Casey*, the 1992 case that many hoped would overturn *Roe v. Wade* (1973). *Roe*, recall, upheld a women's constitutional right to terminate her pregnancy as part of the "liberty" protected by Fourteenth Amendment due process. It was, for many, a sign of a Supreme Court divorced from text and original meaning. In no small part, it helped forge modern originalism. Having passed away two years earlier, Justice Black was no longer on the Court, but his ghost lived on in Justice William Rehnquist's dissenting opinion in *Roe*, which even cited *Lochner* and the ills of "substantive due process." Criticism of *Roe* with its perceived judicial lawmaking became a touchstone of originalist thinking and jurisprudence.[18]

Yet in a plurality opinion, the Supreme Court in *Casey* upheld the "central holding" of *Roe*— recognizing a woman's liberty to terminate her pregnancy, particularly in the early months. Scalia's dissent was a lucid and elegant articulation of how the Court should interpret the liberty protected by due process; it would govern his understanding for the rest of his days. Scalia argued that the liberty to terminate a pregnancy may well be of interest to many women, but it was not found in the Constitution. And that was the only question for the Court. "The issue is whether it is a liberty protected by the Constitution of the United States. I am sure it is not. I reach that conclusion . . . for the same reason I reach the conclusion that bigamy is not constitutionally protected—because of two simple facts: (1) the Constitution says absolutely nothing about it, and (2) the longstanding traditions of American society have permitted it to be legally proscribed."[19]

Following Justice Black, Scalia argued that the liberties protected by Fourteenth Amendment due process include the rights listed in the Bill of Rights by way of incorporation.[20] But Scalia added an important wrinkle: liberties rooted in history. In this, Scalia draws on Black's great antagonist, Justice Felix Frankfurter. Whereas Frankfurter spoke to "canons of decency" and "standards of justice" that suggested a more open-ended and evolving history, Scalia turned to tradition to discern clearly identifiable rights. Rights that had long been protected by American's conception of due process could be included because they could be clearly identified by history. Indeed, Scalia's critique of unenumerated rights sounds remarkably like Justice Black's: "All manner of 'liberties,' the Court tells us, inhere in the Constitution and are enforceable by this Court—not just those mentioned in the text or established by the traditions of our society. Why even the Ninth Amendment—which says only that 'the enumeration in the Constitution of certain rights shall not be construed to deny or disparage others retained by the people'—is, despite our contrary understanding for almost 200 years, a literally boundless source of additional, unnamed, unhinted-at 'rights,' definable and enforceable by us, through 'reasoned' judgment."[21]

Scalia's arguments for text and tradition are rooted in the same sort of arguments Justice Black made: Text and tradition limit judicial discretion. If judges stick to rights clearly enumerated in constitutional text by reading liberty in the Fourteenth Amendment to refer to rights enumerated in the Bill of Rights, they will be tethered to the text. Tradition, for Scalia, operates in a similar fashion: "texts and traditions are facts to study." They ground judicial will. In comparison, if we open up textual provisions like the Ninth Amendment, if we think of liberties not rooted firmly in tradition, we risk allowing judicial discretion to engage in the wholesale creation of rights. A seminal figure in the development of originalism and textualism situated between Black and Scalia, Judge Robert Bork insisted that "the judge who looks outside the Constitution always looks inside himself and nowhere else."[22] For Scalia, text and tradition informed by original meaning offered the judge an objective standard of interpretation, making it more likely to cabin the errant impulse to judicial creation.

Democracy and the Judiciary

Scalia's understanding of text and originalism was deeply rooted in his understanding of democratic self-government. Rights marked off in constitutional text remove them from the democratic process and enable the judiciary to protect them. Yet this also allows democratic majorities to govern where rights are not marked off by way of textual enumeration. Enumerated rights are bestowed with legal significance and protected by courts. Everything else is subject to democratic debate and persuasion. Many of the most pressing questions in our democracy must be settled by efforts to persuade your fellow citizens. That is the nature of democracy. It is only when an original act of the people set aside certain rights that they were insulated from the democratic process and protected by courts. Steven Calabresi—a former law clerk to Justice Scalia, founding member of the Federalist Society, and leading originalist scholar—goes so far to argue, "Justice Scalia's theorizing about constitutional interpretation must be read with this democratic lodestar in mind."[23] Protecting unenumerated rights in cases like *Griswold*, *Roe*, and *Casey*, perverts the judicial role because it tramples on the peoples' right to democratic self-government. Scalia's understanding of democracy shapes his understanding of constitutional text.

Scalia highlighted this argument in due process cases. In *Lawrence v. Texas* (2003), the Court held that a Texas statue prohibiting homosexual sodomy (but not heterosexual sodomy) was an unconstitutional deprivation of liberty under the Fourteenth Amendment's due process clause. The Court's reasons for doing so were not as lucid as they might have been. Justice Anthony Kennedy's opinion for the Court held that Texas had no rational reason for regulating homosexual conduct in a manner that it did not regulate heterosexual conduct—other than to express moral disapproval. But, according to Kennedy, a jurist also appointed by President Reagan shortly after he appointed Scalia, that's not a legitimate state interest. Justice Kennedy's ponderous and overwrought prose often obscured his logic; yet his argument pointed to the idea that due process protected individuals from arbitrary discrimination that could not be connected to a *legitimate* state interest. Why punish homosexual sodomy but not heterosexual sodomy? Kennedy expanded on this logic in finding prohibitions on same-sex marriage unconstitutional. The general logic has roots in earlier Fourteenth Amendment jurisprudence, which declined to specify liberty in all its particular phases but held that states could not deprive citizens of liberty based on arbitrary classifications or regulations. We saw this sort of argument in *Meyer v. Nebraska* (1923), where the Court held it unconstitutional to prohibit teaching the German language to school-aged children, arguing the prohibition was an arbitrary regulation based on animus to Germans rather than a legitimate regulation aimed to promote the public welfare. Numerous cases after the Civil War embraced this logic, and it has been defended on originalist grounds.[24] Kennedy's opinion played up the fact that animus alone was driving the Texas prohibition of homosexual sodomy.

Scalia would have none of it. He argued that the Fourteenth Amendment "expressly allows States to deprive their citizens of 'liberty,' so long as 'due process of law' is provided."[25] So what constitutes due process? In the vast majority of cases, Scalia argued, it is simply a matter of allowing the democratic process to play out. The Court's only concern should be whether the law at issue *potentially* serves a "reasonable" state interest. This case easily met that standard—maintaining traditional sexual mores was a perfectly rational action on the part of Texas. It was only when "fundamental liberty interests" were at stake that the Court should subject laws to a higher level of scrutiny: "We have held repeatedly, in cases the Court today does not overrule, that only fundamental rights qualify for this so-called 'heightened scrutiny' protection—that is, rights which are 'deeply rooted in the Nation's history and tradition.'"[26] For Scalia, these rights primarily included rights enumerated in the Bill of Rights, and nothing there said anything about a right to engage in homosexual sodomy. But Scalia also looked to history, noting that homosexual conduct had long been prohibited in American society dating back to the founding. Thus, "the conclusion that homosexual sodomy is not a fundamental right 'deeply rooted in this Nation's history and tradition' is utterly unassailable."[27]

Echoing his arguments from *Casey*, Scalia insisted that because there was not a fundamental right to engage in homosexual sodomy, it could be regulated and prohibited by the democratic process. Worse, the Court's intervention deprived the people of their right to govern themselves. In contrast to the democratic process, which leaves open the chance to persuade your fellow citizens, Scalia noted that the Court's "deeply illiberal opinion" imposes, by fiat, its moral view on the democratic majority. Scalia reiterated this argument in cases dealing with same-sex marriage: "Few public controversies will ever demonstrate so vividly the beauty of what our Framers gave us, a gift the Court pawns today to buy its stolen moment in the spotlight: a system of government that permits us to rule ourselves."[28]

Limiting Text

I want to bring out Scalia's unwritten assumptions more fully because they are not obvious. Nor are they always consistent with constitutional text. This is most evident regarding open-ended constitutional provisions like the due process clause. When it comes to due process, Scalia does not clearly turn to original public meaning or historical debates surrounding the ratification of the Fourteenth Amendment. For all the rich debate around the framing of the Fourteenth Amendment, Scalia has neither drawn on it nor contributed to it. Rather, like Justice Black, he looks to specified rights in order to limit judicial interpretation. Unlike Black, he thinks these can be rooted in tradition as well as in text: "we have insisted not merely that the interest denominated as a 'liberty' be 'fundamental' (a concept that, in isolation, is hard to objectify), but also that it be an interest traditionally protected by our society."[29] Yet he reads constitutional text and tradition through the lens of limiting judicial discretion. Limiting judicial discretion, however, is a feature of his understanding of democracy; it is not derived from constitutional text. Even more, when it comes to statutory interpretation—ordinary written laws—Scalia insists on the plain meaning of the text. It is the text that is the law and not the intent of those who authored the text. Yet Scalia often rejects plain meaning textualism when it comes to the Constitution. "Words in the Constitution," Scalia argues, are "not to be interpreted in the abstract, but rather according to the understandings that existed when they were adopted."[30]

Indeed, Scalia wants to close open-ended readings of textual provisions because he fears they are invitations to the judicial creation of rights. Scalia made this evident during oral argument in *McDonald v. Chicago* (2010). In the spring of 2010, the Supreme Court heard arguments about whether the Second Amendment right to "bear arms" applied to the states by way of the Fourteenth Amendment. In 2008, Justice Scalia wrote an opinion for the Court in *District of Columbia v. Heller* holding on originalist grounds that the Second Amendment protected an individual right to bears arms. *Heller*, however, did not answer the question of whether this right found in the Second Amendment also found expression in the Fourteenth Amendment and, thereby, applied to the states. This very question was before the Court in *McDonald*. But it was given an interesting twist. Lead counsel for those who challenged the Chicago ordinance, Alan Gura, insisted that the right to bear arms was rooted in the original meaning of the Fourteenth Amendment's privileges or immunities clause. This position was supported by leading originalists across the political spectrum.

Scalia did not bite. Indeed, he was altogether dismissive of the argument. He wanted to know why we should attempt to return to the original meaning of the privileges or immunities clause, given that it was at odds with over 100 years of Supreme Court precedent—even if it was also widely acknowledged that this precedent was wrong. With some contempt, Scalia asked if counsel was "bucking for a place—a place on some law school faculty" as, he noted, the "privileges or immunities clause is the darling of the professoriate." It's interesting for a putative textualist to be so dismissive of text. It's interesting that a putative originalist is so dismissive of originalism. Yet it fits with Scalia's understanding of text and originalism if we understand both in terms of *limiting judicial discretion*. This, too, came out in oral argument. Peppered with questions about the privileges or immunities of citizenship, Mr. Gura admitted, as many before him had, that it was difficult to give a "full description of all unenumerated rights" that might be protected by the Fourteenth Amendment under the privileges or immunities clause. Justice Scalia quipped, "Doesn't that trouble you?"[31] Not only does it trouble Scalia, it also drives both his textualism and his originalism. The organizing principle of Scalia's jurisprudence is the need to obviate judicial willfulness within democratic self-government. This is what leads him to text and tradition.

Scalia's understanding of democracy is quite simplistic. In an address at Gregorian University in Rome, Scalia insisted "the whole theory of democracy is that the majority rules; that is the whole theory of it." He then insisted the "minority loses, except to the extent that the majority, in its document of government, has agreed to accord the minority rights."[32] Scalia's critics, including originalist critics, often disagree with his interpretation of constitutional text because they think he is foundationally wrong in his reading of democracy, casting the complex form of constitutional democracy the Constitution embraces as a simple form of majoritarian democracy in a manner that distorts his reading of constitutional text. In this way, Scalia wants to limit potentially open-ended or more general constitutional clauses to hedge in the judiciary and allow democratic majorities to rule. His critics think the version of constitutional democracy that underlies the Constitution may well empower courts to articulate and protect rights rooted in the more open-ended and abstract clauses.[33] Scalia downplays such views from the founding and Civil War era in favor of a more populist form of democracy. The quarrel between Scalia and his antagonists often turns on which version of democracy the Constitution embraces, and how the judiciary should be situated within that understanding.[34]

Scalia is concerned that judges should not be given too much discretion lest they engage in judicial "lawmaking." In a democracy, judges ought to defer to legislatures unless they have a very clear reason in constitutional text to reject acts of the legislature. This is a powerful argument. To reiterate, it's an argument that depends on Scalia's understanding of democracy and the proper role of the judiciary in a democracy; it is not evident from constitutional text. In fact, as we can see, Scalia could be outright dismissive of constitutional text when it potentially invited a more abstract role for the Court, even if it was one potentially grounding in the founders' understanding of constitutional democracy and articulated even more fully by those who framed the Fourteenth Amendment.

The privileges or immunities clause in the Fourteenth Amendment may have been deliberately framed to avoid enumerating specific rights. As Senator Jacob Howard of Michigan said in the debates framing the amendment: "To these privileges and immunities, whatever they may be—for they are not and cannot be fully defined in their entire extent and precise nature—to these should be added the personal rights guarantied and secured by the first eight amendments to the Constitution."[35] In making this argument, Senator Howard turned to Bushrod Washington's opinion in *Corfield v. Coryell* (1823), as did a number of other members of Congress during the framing debates in both the House and the Senate.[36] Those who framed the amendment insisted that civil liberties included what have often been referred to as long-standing rights at common law—the right to follow a trade, contract, own property, bring suit in court, and habeas corpus—as well as natural rights forged in early American constitutionalism—the right to freedom of speech, freedom of the press, freedom of assembly, and freedom of religion.

With the passage of the Fourteenth Amendment a host of civil liberties that had remained insecure were now secured against the states and rooted in national citizenship. If such rights were not always clearly specified, they were not simply malleable: A judge could not read whatever he or she wanted into the "privileges or immunities" of citizenship. Admittedly, there was hesitation to specify them "in their entire extent" for reasons that were remarkably similar to the arguments against a bill of rights that we saw in the last chapter. And yet, following Scalia, if we turn to history and tradition, we find these rights extolled again and again in the antebellum years—and throughout the debates on the Civil Rights Act of 1866 and the Fourteenth Amendment—even if they were constitutionally insecure prior to the ratification of that amendment. Yet Scalia was reluctant, at best, to recognize such rights as attaching to citizenship, despite their being recognized by history and pointed to by text—particularly in originalist scholarship.[37]

I want to pause on an important point here regarding originalist scholarship. Scalia argues for the original meaning as understood by those who ratified the Constitution compared to those who drafted it. Recall that this debate is characterized as a debate between "original meaning" (ratifiers' intent) and "original intent" (framers' intent). But with the Civil War amendments—the Thirteenth, Fourteenth, and Fifteenth—there is very little in the way of historical debate to draw on to determine ratifiers' intent. As it happens, this is somewhat true of the Bill of Rights as well. While the debate over the Constitution and whether it should include a bill of rights is rich and detailed, the ratification debates over the amendments that ultimately became the Bill of Rights is fairly thin. So is the ratification debate over the Fourteenth Amendment. In these cases, framers' intent may become more important, even if it's used in a manner to help construct a likely vision of ratifiers' intent. While originalism began as a deeply historical enterprise, turning to history to understand what the "author" of the text was conveying, in its new form, which began partly with Scalia, it is much less historical and much more linguistic and philosophical.[38] What has been dubbed "original public meaning" turns on elucidating what the Constitution's words would have meant to an ordinary reader at the time of its enactment.[39] Original public meaning turns on analyzing dictionaries and linguistic conventions from the historical period under investigation, not on actual historical analysis of the ratification debates let alone historical analysis of the political controversies and debates that drove the framing of such constitutional provisions.[40] Originalists give priority to text based on grammar more than history, as Justice Barrett notes, "because they believe that *it and it alone is law*."[41]

Original Meanings and Original Applications

Constitutional text does not tell us which originalist approach, if any, is required. Nor does text instruct us at what level of abstraction we should read textual provisions even when we are attempting to follow the original understanding of those who ratified the Constitution. Consider the case of *Loving v. Virginia* (1967). Virginia had long prohibited interracial marriage. Does forbidding, in the language of the day, "white persons" from intermarrying "colored persons" and "colored persons" from intermarrying "white persons" violate the equal protection clause? If we begin with the text itself—no state shall deprive any person of the equal protection of the law—we have to ask whether a law that prohibits both whites from marrying blacks and blacks from marrying whites is consistent with any sense of equality. Inevitably, that raises important questions the text does not answer. This is why Scalia argues we should limit our textual inquiry to the original meaning of the text—to what those who ratified the text thought it meant. But questions linger.

Put aside for a moment how we determine the original meaning of the text and focus, instead, on how abstractly or concretely we should understand original meaning. Is the question for us, in 1967 when the Supreme Court decided *Loving*, what did those who ratified the Fourteenth Amendment think about interracial marriage? Is it what did those who ratified the Fourteenth Amendment think about racial discrimination? Is it what did those who ratified the amendment think about the nature of liberty and equality? Early versions of originalism—whether focusing on framers' intent or ratifiers' intent—insisted on the concrete understandings behind intent. If the framers' or ratifiers' understanding of equal protection would not have prohibited bans on interracial marriage, as in the case of *Loving*, then the equal protection clause would not extend to these issues. Constitutional text, in this sense, is defined by the original *application* and *expectations* of those who framed or ratified the text. You can see the appeal of this approach if you consider that early originalists were preoccupied by confining judicial discretion: Concrete expectations limit our interpretation of text. Yet this understanding of originalism has fallen out of scholarly fashion.[42]

Many originalists today agree that we should not limit ourselves to the particular expectations of those who ratified the text. If the original public meaning of the text was understood to promise racial equality, we should apply that understanding whatever the particular expectations of those who ratified the text. This gets a bit abstract. Think of it this way. Even if those who ratified the amendment thought the promise of racial equality was perfectly consistent with segregated schools and prohibitions on interracial marriage, we should not be governed by their particular *expectations* regarding racial equality. Despite the fact that prohibitions on interracial marriage were widespread at the time of the ratification of the Fourteenth Amendment, and persisted until late into the twentieth century, those particular *expectations* of what racial equality entailed do not govern our interpretation of the Fourteenth Amendment. We are not concerned with how those who ratified the Fourteenth Amendment *applied* it in particular cases; nor are we concerned with how they *expected* it to apply. We are concerned with what racial equality commands based on the ratifiers' more general understanding of equal protection. That's why Justice Scalia can insist that prohibitions on interracial marriage have been unconstitutional since 1868—the year the Fourteenth Amendment was ratified.[43]

Why? Because at its core, the original public meaning of the Fourteenth Amendment prohibited the government from creating distinctions rooted in race. Including racially segregated schools and railcars, even if they did not expect the Fourteenth Amendment to apply to these issues and even if as originally applied it did not.[44] The original public meaning of equal protection commands that *Brown v. Board of Education* (1954), which found that racially segregated public schools were unconstitutional, is right and that *Plessy v. Ferguson* (1896), which held that segregated railcars were constitutionally permissible, is wrong.[45] It matters not a whit that, historically speaking, the people who actually ratified the amendment might have thought that racial segregation was consistent with equal protection. They were wrong.

Once we are liberated from concrete expectations, from the particular historical application of racial equality, and governed by the principle put in play, we still have to ask at what level of abstraction. Does the equal protection clause apply only to racial equality? Does it apply to other categories? If so, which ones? Considering Scalia's due process opinions regarding discrimination against homosexuality, he turns to *history*, though not necessarily on originalist grounds, to limit judicial interpretation to concrete examples. Yet when he turns to questions of racial equality—whether it is racially segregated schools, railcars, or prohibitions on interracial marriage—he appeals to a more general principle of racial equality that spurns the particular history. There is a tension between an understanding of originalism that is largely negative—that is, confining judicial interpretation—and an understanding of originalism that is largely positive—that is, faithfully interpreting the Constitution. Justice Barrett helpfully notes this shift: "Originalism has shifted from being a theory about how judges should decide cases to a theory about what counts as valid, enforceable law."[46]

Scalia straddles this divide: Originalism as a "lesser evil" leans toward the first wave of originalism, whereas the turn to original meaning divorced from concrete expectations paved the way for the second wave of originalism. Originalism in this second wave has many varieties.[47] Original meaning could be based on extracting the principled understanding of those who participated in historical debates over the amendment, or it could be about extracting the linguistic understanding of equality and what it would have meant to a reasonable person at the time. I don't wish to get bogged down in the intricacies of these debates. However derived, we must still grapple with the question of what level of generality we are bound by in applying original meaning.[48]

Put simply: If the Fourteenth Amendment put forward a principle of equal protection, do we use that as a general principle for all cases or only racial equality? Or somewhere in between? To return to Scalia: Why is he so sure that original meaning prohibits bans on interracial marriage but equally sure it does not forbid prohibitions of same-sex marriage?

Originalism and Levels of Generality

Scalia does not address this question head on. He insists that we are not concerned with *current understandings* of equality but the original understanding. But just as surely, we are not limited to the *concrete expectations* of those who ratified the Fourteenth Amendment's equal protection clause. In an exchange with the legal and constitutional philosopher Ronald Dworkin, Scalia denied that he was a "time-dated" originalist—that is, wed to particular expectations—and insisted he was governed by the "semantic meaning" of the text.[49] In providing for equal protection with regard to race, we may have to apply the Fourteenth Amendment in ways that are at odds with the particular expectations of those who ratified the amendment.

For Scalia, what is clear about the original meaning of the equal protection clause is that it prohibited racial discrimination. The original meaning of the Fourteenth Amendment would thus prohibit racial classifications that treated black Americans unequally.[50] Even if when the Fourteenth Amendment was ratified, the District of Columbia, governed by Congress, segregated schools on the basis of race, that practice does not define the original meaning of the amendment. So it is with laws prohibiting interracial marriage. Such laws, and the practice of some forms of segregation, illustrate that those who ratified the amendment may have expected that equal protection did not prohibit such practices. But those expectations are wrong: They are at odds with the promise of racial equality.[51] Interpreting the Constitution in our time, we are governed by the original public meaning of the text, not the original expectations about what that meaning required. Interpreting original meaning requires us to apply the text at a more general level, abstracting from concrete expectations. At least with regard to race.

Yet notice, again, that Scalia limits text primarily to racial issues when the text itself imposes no such limitation. In Scalia's hands, the text would read something like "no state shall deprive any person of equal protection of the laws on the basis of race." He rejects concrete expectations with regard to segregated schools and anti-miscegenation laws—allowing him to justify *Brown* and *Loving* on originalist grounds—but he quickly retreats to a "'time-dated' meaning of equal protection in 1868 when moving beyond race.[52] When it comes to discrimination on the basis of gender, such distinctions are perfectly fine under the Fourteenth Amendment because, based on the understanding of those who ratified the amendment, the "equal protection of the laws" did not prohibit discrimination on the basis of gender.[53] It's perfectly fine for society to alter these forms of discrimination by way of legislation, but it is not constitutionally required based on the original meaning and so should not be judicially enforced. But why reject a "time-dated" understanding with regard to race, while insisting on it when moving beyond race?

Contrary to Scalia, originalist scholars—like University of Chicago law professor William Baude and Northwestern University law professor Steven Calabresi—argue that the original meaning of the equal protection clause put forward an anti-caste principle that prohibited arbitrary classifications among citizens. This principle applies most powerfully and obviously to questions of racial discrimination. Yet just because the ratifiers of the amendment did not think to apply this principle to discrimination on the basis of gender or sexual orientation, does not make their expectations definitive. A concept, standard, or principle set in motion by an earlier generation can entail obligations they could not anticipate. We are applying the *principle* they brought into being, not their *expectations* for that principle. As Calabresi explains: "The Framers and ratifiers of the Fourteenth Amendment [did not] understand sex discrimination to be a form of caste . . . legislation . . . but sometimes legislators misapply or misunderstand their own rules."[54] Or they just don't consider issues that later generations consider because of their perhaps misguided assumptions. Not only does the equal protection clause apply to gender on originalist grounds, but it also applies to sexual orientation. Baude and Calabresi argue that *Obergefell* (the same-sex marriage case), for example, can be defended on originalist grounds.[55]

Like Scalia, they reject a "time-dated" understanding of original meaning. Those who framed the Fourteenth Amendment did not think it would apply to anything like same-sex marriage. They never for a moment thought of such questions. Despite their expectations, the principled understanding of equal protection they brought into being forbids prohibitions on same-sex marriage rooted in arbitrary classifications just as it prohibits racially segregated schools rooted in arbitrary classifications. The principled understanding of the original meaning treats these categories at an abstract level. The constitutional text applies to circumstances its ratifiers never imagined—discrimination on the basis of sexual orientation—and does so on originalist grounds.[56]

Scalia would have none of this. Yet his reasons for doing so point back to the tensions in his textualism and originalism. As we have seen in his due process jurisprudence and defense of originalism as the "lesser evil," Scalia turns to concrete historical understandings to limit judicial interpretation of constitutional text. Here he embraces "time-dated" understandings. Many subsequent originalists are much more open to interpretation rooted in the principles and values of constitutional clauses. We see this in the arguments of many leading originalists who insist that we must draw out abstract principles or commands from the constitutional text. Is this so different from Scalia's application of principles regarding freedom of speech and the press to circumstances those who ratified the First Amendment never thought about or could not have known about?[57] No one who ratified the First Amendment could conceive of radio, television, or the internet. Yet, Scalia argues, the principles rooted in the First Amendment apply to these mediums. Radio, television, and the personal computer are essentially like a book or a newspaper from the late eighteenth century. In a similar fashion, the Fourth Amendment prohibition on "unreasonable searches and seizures" applies to all sorts of technological innovations.[58] The technological development of wire-tapping and other intrusive ways of searching a person cannot be used to get around the principle that prohibits unreasonable searches. Scalia also found that the individual right to own a gun applied with particular force to handguns, even though the handgun did not exist when the Second Amendment was ratified.[59]

Thus questions arise: Is the application of equality to sexual orientation similar to these other interpretive efforts? Is it simply the application of a constitutional rule to a set of circumstances we had not previously considered? Even if we think that constitutional meaning is fixed, does its application change over time? Does this require what Lawrence Lessig, a former clerk to Scalia and Harvard law professor, calls a translation of original meaning to a new context?[60] Our answers to these questions do not turn on text but on our understanding of the kind of democratic government that underlies the Constitution.

***

Despite Scalia's efforts, we cannot escape constitutional judgment by relying on constitutional text and original meaning. Most originalists agree. Even if originalism is about discovering the meaning of fixed constitutional text, most originalists concede that text and original meaning are often underdetermined when it comes to pressing constitutional questions. Indeed, within originalist scholarship there is a distinction between "constitutional interpretation" and "constitutional construction." Within this framework, constitutional interpretation is understood to speak to discernible meaning within the text: Interpretation brings out latent meaning that resides within the text itself.[61] In contrast, constitutional construction is an effort to build out meaning when interpretation alone is not enough. Here meaning must be "determined" rather than "found."[62] At this point, Scalia argues that we should defer to democratically enacted legislation when interpretation "runs out." But this is based on a constitutional construction; that is, we determined, *chose*, that judicial deference to the democratic judgments of the legislature is best when meaning is unclear. Many contemporary originalists—"new originalists"—argue that when discoverable meaning runs out, we can construct meaning from the text and the intentions that we have. Construction, as the Princeton politics professor Keith Whittington argues, works to "carry the Constitution into practice."[63] Randy Barnett argues that "when the abstract terms of the Constitution do not directly resolve a particular dispute, some construction (as opposed to interpretation) of constitutional meaning is needed."[64] Yet such constructions are to be guided by text and what we can discern of original meaning.

Following this, the meaning of "commerce" in Article I, Section 8, may be a question of interpretation. The meaning of Article IV's guarantee of a "republican form of government" may be a question of construction. The most prominent advocates of this distinction acknowledge the boundary between interpretation and construction can be blurry. Even so, construction should be something turned to as a supplement to interpretation. Whether this distinction is persuasive will come up in later chapters.[65] I flag the distinction here to note that something akin to constitutional construction pervades debate about constitutional interpretation. Consider Scalia's understanding of what level of judicial scrutiny to apply to "fundamental rights." Or, for that matter, how to determine whether a right is fundamental. These—and many, many more understandings that we have and will encounter— are best seen as built out from constitutional text rather than determined by it.

Early constitutional debates used the terms interpretation and construction interchangeably. Maybe that's best. Yet, however we think of constitutional constructions, they do not simply supplement constitutional interpretation. They frequently drive it, as we've seen with Scalia. We might think of these as interpretations that draw out the essential nature and logic of the Constitution, or we might think of them as constructions that build out constitutional meaning. Either way, we are turning to unwritten understandings that sketch a form of political theory to best comprehend the Constitution. And it is this *theory that guides our reading* of discrete textual clauses. The sort of judicial scrutiny we apply to particular rights is determined by our *constructions* of judicial power and constitutional self-government. When we disagree on which rights are entitled to what level of judicial scrutiny, we are disagreeing about unwritten constructions of the Constitution. Going forward, I refer to constructions when ideas and concepts are not simply determined by constitutional text but are being used in a way to frame our reading of the text.

There are originalists who deny that there is a crucial difference between constitutional interpretation and constitutional construction, and originalists who deny the legitimacy of construction.[66] Is judicial review, which is not clearly spelled out in text, a result of drawing out latent meaning (interpretation), or is it a necessary construction rooted in the structure and logic of the Constitution? It is an interesting and important debate that we will return to in chapter 5. It's a debate, though, like many of the sophisticated debates within the scholarly world of originalism, that has almost no purchase at all in the political sphere or among originalist judges (though perhaps that will change as originalism becomes more pervasive on the Court). In political and public debates, the somewhat caricatured version of Scalia as a "strict constructionist" who sticks to text holds sway as the primary understanding of originalism. An understanding that Scalia himself nurtured in his later years.

My deeper point is that construction is always occurring—and always necessary—at some level. Even if we think the judiciary should only engage in interpretation and discover the plain meaning of the text, we're doing so because of our construction of the role of the judiciary within the constitutional scheme. Even if we attempt to circumscribe judicial authority by arguing that courts should only overturn democratically enacted legislation when such legislation clearly violates the original public meaning of the text as understood by the concrete expectations of those who ratified the text, we are inevitably resting our arguments on some form or another of constitutional construction. We are constructing rules and understandings to guide the judiciary based on our overall understanding of what we think the Constitution is and was meant to do. We see such constructions from the earliest moments in our history, which I take up in the next chapter.

3

Text and Republican Government

Let's return to one of the Supreme Court's first opinions, Justice Samuel Chase's in *Calder v. Bull* (1798). I begin with Chase's opinion in *Calder* because it is often taken by textualists to be representative of non-textual interpretation, a textbook example of illegitimate constitutional interpretation, or "judicial lawmaking," even if Chase happened to decide the case correctly. As Justice Black suggested in *Griswold v. Connecticut* (1965), the contraception case that identified a constitutional right to privacy, Chase was engaged in "natural law" theorizing, departing from constitutional text, to read his moral and philosophical dispositions into the Constitution. Chase was, to be sure, one of the more colorful characters from the founding generation. He signed the Declaration of Independence, he was appointed to the Supreme Court by George Washington, and he is the only Supreme Court justice to ever be impeached by Congress (though he was not removed). Chase was cantankerous and intemperate. Yet Chase's opinion is distorted when viewed through the lens of Justice Black's vision. Read with an open mind, attending to the argument itself, it is possible to see that Chase was engaged in constitutional interpretation of the text, which necessarily drew on a larger understanding of the American constitutional enterprise. Indeed, speaking clearly to textual provisions of the Constitution that depend on unwritten understandings, Chase may help illustrate that turning to the specific underpinnings of American government is not the same as turning to "natural law" or moral and philosophical principles on their own terms.

Calder took up the definition of an ex post facto law. The Connecticut legislature had set aside a court decree and granted a new hearing to resolve a dispute over a will. The question was whether the prohibition against ex post facto laws in Article I, Section 10 of the Constitution applied to all retrospective legislation or only to retrospective legislation with regard to criminal law that inflicted a penalty. The probate

The (Un)Written Constitution. George Thomas, Oxford University Press. © Oxford University Press 2021.
DOI: 10.1093/oso/9780197555972.003.0004

court had awarded Calder and his wife property in a dispute over a will. The Connecticut legislature passed a law setting aside this decree, and therefore voiding Calder's claim to the property while granting a new hearing. In doing this, the legislature divested Calder of the property, which then reverted to Bull and his wife. Calder sued, claiming the law was an ex post facto law insofar as it deprived him of property the probate court had awarded him.

In discerning the nature of an ex post facto law, Chase insisted: "I cannot subscribe to the omnipotence of a State Legislature, or that it is absolute and without control; although its authority should not be expressly restrained by the Constitution, or fundamental law, of the State."[1] This passage is one of two that are plausible references to natural law or natural justice. Yet Chase proceeds to speak specifically to the American state constitutions to situate his understanding. He appeals to neither natural law nor natural justice. Rather, he turns to the particulars of American constitutions.[2] Indeed, just after this passage he speaks to why the people of the United States erected *their* constitutions, insisting that the "purposes for which men enter into society will determine the nature and terms of the social compact." And this is so, Chase argues, because the "foundation of the legislative power" flows from the terms of the social compact. The terms of the American social compact embrace certain "vital principles" in our "free Republican governments" that both determine the extent of legislative power and render certain exercises of such power illegitimate.[3]

Notice that Chase says nothing about natural law or moral principles "outside" of the Constitution. On the contrary, Chase says that the very particulars of why the American people organized their constitutions on the principles that they did will determine the limit and reach of state power. Wouldn't it be striking if it were otherwise? Chase does not say these principles must coincide with natural justice or natural law. In some accounts of these abstract concepts, the American constitutions might in fact overlap—wholly or in part— with a particular version of natural justice or natural law. But that is not what Chase is speaking of. Chase is speaking of the "vital republican principles" that these *particular* constitutions embrace. Chase does insist, with more rhetorical flourish than is necessary, "an ACT of the Legislature (for I cannot call it a law) contrary to the great first principles of the social compact, cannot be considered a rightful exercise of legislative authority."[4] It is this line that, more than anything else, has led to charges that Chase is engaged in natural law reasoning. Yet it is far from clear this is what Chase is up to. On the contrary, if this line refers to the particulars of the American Constitution (including the state constitutions) as a social compact between the people, it is a commonsense statement that all constitutional interpreters would immediately agree on—whatever their theory of constitutional interpretation. What Chase really seems to be saying is that an *unconstitutional* law cannot bind us. And that is because the legislature did not have the constitutional authority to enact it. So an unconstitutional law cannot really be a law. Not because it is against "natural justice" or a particular moral philosophy, but because it is at odds with the social compact that underlies America's *written* Constitution.

Chase does have references to "reason" and "justice" and to the "genius, the nature, and the spirit of our State Constitutions." And he does say that the powers of the federal and state legislatures are limited even if they are not always expressly restrained. Yet Justice Chase does not say these limits are because of natural justice: They flow from the very nature of America's *republican* constitutional enterprise. The grants of legislative power from the people are not unlimited in a republican government. It is incumbent on the legislature to justify its use of power. Chase's rhetoric may well be less restrained than we would prefer from a jurist; it certainly is prone to lofty pronouncements of grand principles. And Chase, as we will see later, could be astonishingly intemperate. Perhaps he can be excused in that he was seeking to impart these principles in the public mind, even if he was over the top in doing so. References to reason and to the nature and to the logic of the thing are littered throughout *The Federalist Papers*. Such references refer to the purpose of a written constitution and point to the principles and ideas that are necessary to make sense of it.[5] Justice Scalia himself, much like Chase, refers to cannons of reason necessary to judicial interpretation.[6] Chase turned to these background principles, to the political theory behind written constitutions in America, rooted in what he referred to as the fundamental principles of the social compact, as an essential feature of constitutional interpretation. As Justice Chase puts it, "I am under a necessity to give a *construction*, or explanation of the words 'ex post facto laws,' because they have not any certain meaning attached to them."[7]

Such constructions are an essential part of interpreting America's written Constitution. We cannot make sense of our written Constitution without them. At times this does require, as Chase argued, understanding the very nature and purpose of the social compact—the kind of republican government the written Constitution brought into being. We see this in two early cases of constitutional interpretation/ construction that speak to the very nature of the American constitutional order, to the political theory behind America's republican experiment, to make sense of textual provisions. The first case is Article VI's prohibition of religious tests for office. The second is freedom of speech and the press in the First Amendment.

Religious Liberty and the Logic of the Constitution

In considering the proposed constitution in 1788, the North Carolina Ratifying Convention took up the meaning of an often-overlooked clause of Article VI. Beyond making the Constitution the supreme law of the land, Article VI requires that all public officials, federal and state, swear an oath to support the Constitution. It then commands: "no religious test shall ever be required as a qualification to any office or public trust under the United States." The clause points to religious liberty, which is also seen in the textual provision that allows an "affirmation" to support the Constitution in place of an oath; an acknowledgment that some religions object to taking an oath. This short textual provision rests on deep principles.

As often happens, it was an objection to the clause that brought out its deeper meaning. The Reverend David Caldwell, a Princeton-educated Presbyterian minister, worried that the prohibition on religious tests stood as "an invitation for Jews and pagans of every kind to come among us." This would change the future character of the United States. Given this, he objected to ratifying the Constitution, insisting that the "gentlemen who formed this Constitution should not have given this 'invitation to Jews and heathens.'"[8] It would invite them into

America—and to hold public office—undermining America's political and religious morality. The Reverend Caldwell was offering an alternative vision of political order: a Protestant republic or, at least, a Christian one.

James Iredell, whom George Washington would later appoint to the Supreme Court, agreed with Reverend Caldwell, but took it on himself to explain why this indicated a monumental development to be embraced rather than rejected. He explained the nature and logic of religious liberty and toleration as essential features of the political order that America had brought into being. This was, keep in mind, prior to the First Amendment's guarantee of religious liberty and separation of church and state, as the amendment was not proposed and ratified until 1791, three years later. This is also the same Iredell whom Justice Black would draw on as his guide to "constitutional philosophy" in *Griswold*.

Iredell began by confessing shock that the clause raised such objections. He then quickly acknowledged that non-Christians were equal citizens and could hold public office. The clause, Iredell argued, should be understood as part of a deeper sense of religious liberty in America, highlighting the novelty of the American experiment. Looking to recent history, religious tests were used in cruel ways to block members of nonconforming religions from holding office and, while tolerating them, degrading them from the rank of equal citizens. The result was a history of religious strife and warfare where "each church has in turn set itself up against every other." In contrast, "America has set an example to mankind to think more modestly and reasonably—that a man may be of different religious sentiments from our own, without being a bad member of society."[9]

Iredell pointed to the clause as "one of the strongest proofs that could be adduced, that it was the intention of those who formed this system to establish a general religious liberty in America." But this was not, as some might contend, religious liberty among various Protestant sects. Nor was it toleration in the old sense; that is, following the British Acts of Toleration, a grant of religious liberty to nonconforming sects that remained consistent with denying nonconforming sects public office, as well as admittance to Oxford and Cambridge Universities, making it exquisitely clear that they were not viewed as equal citizens but *merely* tolerated. In the American sense, Iredell argued, toleration meant equal religious liberty. "Happily," in America, "no sect here is superior to another. As long as this is the case, we shall be free from those persecutions and distractions with which other countries have been torn."[10] The prohibition on religious tests for public office indicated central principles of political theory with regard to church and state: the "article is calculated to secure universal religious liberty, by putting all sects on a level—the only way to prevent persecution."[11]

At a time when American was pervasively Protestant and toleration was often limited to various forms of Protestantism, Iredell extended the notion of religious liberty to all. According to the Constitution, full citizenship and equal rights extended to all regardless of religion: "pagans" and "Mahometans," Jews and Catholics, could hold public office. As the historian Denise Spellberg notes, this was hardly likely in 1788 when America was overwhelming Protestant.[12] Even so, Iredell essentially made the point that America *was not* a Protestant nation or even a Christian nation. It was a *secular republic* and religious liberty was an essential feature of the social compact that underlay the Constitution. Iredell, an Anglican himself, reminded his countrymen that in Britain, even nonconforming Protestants did not have equal political rights. In the American republican scheme, religious liberty was universal: "how is it possible to exclude any set of men, without taking away that principle of religious freedom which we ourselves so warmly contend for?"[13] Iredell even went so far to say, against exaggerated and sensational objections, that the pope could be elected president under the Constitution. Or, at any rate, the pope could *not be excluded from* the office because he was a Catholic.

Iredell's construction of the meaning of the text drew on, and drew out, the larger principles of the written Constitution. It was an understanding that turned on the purpose of the Constitution and highlighted, in the American sense, how religious liberty was necessarily protected even prior to the ratification of the First Amendment. This also included some form of separation of church and state insofar as constitutional authority rested on secular rather than theological grounds. So, too, did public office and citizenship. It was no coincidence, Iredell argued, that the prohibition on religious tests occurred with the command that all public officers swear an oath to uphold the

Constitution. The Constitution alone was what public officials were bound by; theological authority had no claims on public officials but was the private choice of individuals exercising their religious liberty. If America was hardly the religiously pluralistic country it would become, Iredell showed why this was a distinct possibility given the political theory that underlie the Constitution.

His understanding informed subsequent thinking. George Washington made a similar point two years later in his letter to the Hebrew Congregation at Newport, a year before the ratification of the First Amendment. Echoing Iredell, Washington insisted that Americans can congratulate themselves as a model to the world in that all "possess alike liberty of conscience and immunities of citizenship." Washington continued, speaking to America's republican scheme: "It is now no more that toleration is spoken of as if it were the indulgence of one class of people that another enjoyed the exercise of their inherent natural rights, for, happily, the Government of the United States, which gives to bigotry no sanction, to persecution no assistance, requires only that they who live under its protection should demean themselves as good citizens in giving it on all occasions their effectual support."[14]

Similarly, Justice Joseph Story in his *Commentaries on the Constitution of the United States* would show how the prohibition on religious tests represented a novel departure. The American Constitution not only provided for religious liberty in a way that commanded equal citizenship, it also did not depend on theological authority for its backing.[15] Religious liberty was different than toleration embraced by Britain and expounded by the great common law jurist William Blackstone. If Blackstone was helpful to Americans in understanding parts of their written Constitution—Iredell and Chase both drew on him in *Calder v. Bull* to explain the prohibition on ex post facto laws—he was altogether irrelevant in understanding religious liberty.[16] And this was because the common law embraced a system that allowed for religious tests of office; it was not truly a regime of religious liberty, but one of forbearance. To make sense of this, we have to understand the essence and character of the American Constitution: The text is illuminated by the nature of America's republican experiment, by these unwritten ideas.

Constructing Freedom of Speech and the Press

A decade after the North Carolina Ratifying Convention, the Alien and Sedition Acts of 1798 would invite profound debate on America's vital republican principles and how they informed the written Constitution. It was a debate about the very nature of constitutional self-government. The Alien Act made it easier for the government to deport people and more difficult for recent immigrants who had previously been treated as citizens to exercise the rights of citizenship.[17] The Sedition Act allowed the government to prosecute its critics for seditious libel, effectively criminalizing criticism of the government.[18] Purportedly concerned about being drawn into war, preoccupied by the makeup of recent immigrants, and worried about agitation against the government, Congress passed the acts together to empower the government to preserve itself against such agitation. The Sedition Act made it a crime to write or speak "false, scandalous and malicious" things against the government with the intent to defame it or bring it into contempt or disrepute. Yet the act, unlike the traditional common law of seditious libel, allowed those prosecuted under it to argue for the truth of what they had said or written. Was this consistent with the First Amendment's command, "Congress shall make no law . . . abridging the freedom of speech, or of the press." There was little disagreement about the text but profound disagreement on what it meant.

This was a debate about what "the freedom of speech and the press" entailed; and it was inseparable from what sort of government the written Constitution brought into being. Later textualists like Justice Hugo Black would insist that "no law means no law." But this is not the difficult question. In this early debate, all agreed that no law meant no law. But no law against what? Against "the freedom of speech and the press." But what was the freedom of speech? What was the freedom of the press?[19] Did it include a right to defame political opponents? Did it include a right to bring the government into disrepute? Did it include a right to advocate against government policy? Were such rights only to be exercised during an election?

The text points to concepts that must be situated in political, historical, philosophical, and moral terms. Defenders of the Sedition Act turned to the British common law inheritance as framing the meaning of freedom of speech and the press. Critics rejected this argument for historical, political, philosophical, and practical reasons. The Sedition Act forced Americans to wrestle with the meaning of free speech in their new context. Certainly, there was discussion of free speech and the press prior to the creation and ratification of the Constitution.[20] During both the framing of the Constitution and the ratification debates, there were those who argued that the Constitution needed to protect both freedom of speech and the press. And many state constitutions, like Virginia's, offered such protections.[21] Yet the insistence on protecting freedom of speech rarely specified just what this entailed. Were these understandings consistent with the Sedition Act?

Defenders of the act thought so: They were defending, in their eyes, freedom of speech and the press. Surprisingly, there was little debate during the ratification of the First Amendment in 1791 over just what the freedom of speech and the press meant. Sure, it protected the freedom of speech and the press, but what did that include? The debates over the Sedition Act may best be seen as efforts to construct constitutional meaning: to understand text based on our understanding of what sort of government the written Constitution brought into being. The text alone was of little help. Even Justice Black—for all his textualist insistence that "no law means no law"—agreed that the press could not, say, disclose the movement of troops in a war zone. So either "no law does not mean no law" or such disclosures are not a central part of "the freedom of speech and the press." Either way, we need to refine these sorts of distinctions to arrive at what "the freedom of speech and press" entails. This is precisely what the debate over the Sedition Act was about.

No Prior Restraint: Common Law Construction

It might surprise you to learn that the Sedition Act was widely viewed as consistent with the First Amendment by most sitting Supreme Court justices.[22] Leading American jurists pointed out that the act was more generous than strictly necessary as it allowed for *truth as a defense*. In this, it was argued, "the freedom of speech" under the First

Amendment simply replicated the common law rule that prohibited no *prior restraint* on speech. The government could punish speech, including speech that it found harmed the government's reputation, it just needed to punish the speech once it was published rather than censoring it prior to publication.

This was, by and large, the Federalist's understanding of freedom of speech when the Sedition Act was passed. It was the overwhelming view of the justices on the Supreme Court when prosecutions took place under the Sedition Act, although this was in dispute among some Federalists. Certainly, some justices who were clearly identified as Federalists, like Justice James Wilson—a signer of both the Declaration of Independence and Constitution and one of President Washington's original appointees to the Supreme Court—held views on freedom of speech and republican government that were at odds with the Sedition Act.[23] The term *federalist* was in flux. Defenders of the Constitution of 1787 like James Madison were known as Federalists, but by 1798 they had become Democratic-Republicans. The debate around the Sedition Act was inextricably linked to the development of two political parties vying for control of the government. If there was agreement in 1788 on ratification of the Constitution—where a James Madison and an Alexander Hamilton could unite—there was profound disagreement in the 1790s over the meaning of the new Constitution. The development of America's political parties stemmed in part from issues over constitutional interpretation that turned on unwritten understandings of the political theory the Constitution rested on.

Federalist justices like Samuel Chase and James Iredell turned to the common law jurist William Blackstone to gloss the meaning of the freedom of speech and the press. Both Chase and Iredell argued that punishing seditious libel was entirely consistent with freedom of speech. At the time, Supreme Court justices also sat as circuit court judges—possibly violating the Constitution—and presided over Sedition Act prosecutions. As a sitting judge, Iredell insisted on the constitutionality of the Sedition Act: Given that free republican government was more dependent on the "good opinion of the people" than other forms of government, it was imperative that such a government be able to punish false speech. While he drew on the logic of republican government, much as Chase had in *Calder v. Bull*, he also insisted that Blackstone's understanding of freedom of speech and the press should be presumed unless the First Amendment were "particularly worded" to suggest otherwise. But this was not the case.[24] So, according to Blackstone's understanding, Congress could make laws "respecting the press, provided the law be such as not to *abridge its freedom*."[25] Punishing speech after the fact for harming the government did not abridge this freedom.

Interestingly, as we saw earlier, Iredell rejected Blackstone as a guide to religious liberty because America's republican government rested on a broad understanding of religious liberty that demanded the full rights of citizens regardless of one's religious affiliations. Why Blackstone should be a guide to freedom of speech and the press, but not religious liberty, Iredell did not say. He did note, however, that the Sedition Act was more generous than the common law; it required that speech be *both malicious and false* to be punished. If the writing could be shown to be true, even if it was malicious and brought the government into disrepute, it would be protected. Yet as a presiding judge, Iredell never instructed a jury that a defendant being prosecuted under the act may have been speaking the truth. On the contrary, he denounced the Democratic-Republican defendants on a few occasions for engaging in "malicious falsehood" and "bad sentiments" that were justly punished under the act.[26]

Yet Iredell was tame in instructing juries compared to Justice Chase. We've already seen Chase's penchant for rhetorical excess in *Calder*. His rhetorical excess and partisan zeal when instructing juries as a presiding judge in Sedition Act prosecutions was famous; it was one of the counts against him that Democratic-Republicans later brought in 1804 when he was impeached in the House of Representatives. But the Senate fell a few votes shy of the two-thirds required to remove him. Partisan disputes over speech, the press, sedition, and an impeachment? History may not repeat itself, but it rhymes.

As a judge, Chase presided over two of the most high-profile trials—those of Thomas Cooper and James Callender. Chase readily accepted the Blackstonian understanding of freedom of speech and the press as only prohibiting prior restraint. Chase's argument was not as fully developed as Iredell's, partly because he seemed to think the constitutional issue easily settled on this score. He repeatedly noted that the freedom of the press did not protect "licentious" speech, which, at times, Chase seemed to think meant anything critical of the government. More interesting is Chase's construction of republican government—all the more so as in *Calder* he pointed to the importance of "vital republican principles" that were a necessary part of constitutional interpretation. That was true here as well. As Chase put it, a licentious press was particularly harmful to the republican form of government because it could "corrupt the public opinion . . . and destroy the morals of the people."[27] It was imperative that such speech be punished to protect the government in a republic.

Acting as his own attorney, Cooper, a Jeffersonian educated at Oxford who had come to American from England in 1794, insisted that republican government requires "perfect freedom of discussion of public characters." If this is not allowed, "how [can] the people exercise on rational grounds their elective franchise?"[28] After the trial, where he was found guilty of seditious libel, Cooper published a pamphlet, *An Account of the Trial of Thomas Cooper*, where he worried that the citizens of this country would draw an unfortunate lesson from his trial: "they will hold their tongues, and refrain their pens, on the subject of politics."[29] Cooper did not. He wrote to influence the election of 1800. Influencing the public mind was the core purpose of the writings for which he was being prosecuted. Cooper wrote that Adams was intent on aggrandizing executive power, which included his efforts to restrict "the liberty of speech and the liberty of the press" by multiplying "laws against libel and sedition" and attempting to enforce "doctrines of confidence in the executive."[30] Cooper then pointed to the public acts of Adams along these lines, which included building the navy and a standing army by borrowing money. Cooper contrasted Adams and his actions and statements with President George Washington in a way that was unflattering to Adams. Cooper doubted Adams's capacity to be president.

At his trial Cooper appealed to the jury:

> This country is divided, and almost equally divided, into two grand parties; usually termed, whether properly or improperly, Federalists and Anti-Federalists: and that the governing powers of the country, and ranked in public opinion under the former denomination—of

these divisions, the one wishes to increase, the other to diminish the powers of the Executive; the one thinks that the people, (the Democracy of the country) has too much power, the other, too little influence on the measures of government: the one is friendly, the other hostile, to a standing army and a permanent Navy: the one thinks them necessary to repeal invasions and aggressions from without and commotions within; the other, that a well organized Militia is a sufficient safeguard for all that an army could protect, and that a navy is more dangerous and expensive than any benefit derived from it can compensate: the one, thinks the liberties of our country endangered by the licentiousness, the other, by the restrictions of the President.[31]

Based on this contrast in political parties, Cooper insisted on the truth of his statement. He was speaking to Adams's public acts, not his personal behavior, and did so without malicious intent. The intent, rather, was to highlight political disagreement about public issues— the very essence of republican government. As Cooper put it to his jury, whether his opinions were right or wrong, "I cannot help thinking they would have been better confuted by evidence and argument than by indictment."[32]

Chase and the prosecution didn't buy it. Chase acknowledged the importance of elections to republican government even while insisting that once the government was in power the minority must "surrender up their judgment." Chase went so far to argue that "private opinion must give way to public judgment, or there must be the end of government."[33] Only those whom the nation has chosen by way of elections may weigh in on such questions. To persistently criticize the government with the *improper* motives of influencing the public against it was unacceptable. Chase charged the jury in Cooper's case: Criticism of President Adams "made with the intent to bring the President into contempt and disrepute, and excite against him the hatred of the people" was properly punished by the Sedition Act because it was not constitutionally protected speech. It did not matter that Cooper might think his opinions true, once the government was in power, it was not Cooper's place to shape the public mind against it; it was his place to acquiesce.

Chase did not explain how this worked with the upcoming election of 1800. Cooper argued that ordinary citizens must be in a position to judge government officials, including the president. To insulate the president from criticism was to place him above the law. Cooper might have quoted Adams himself on republican government from the Massachusetts Constitution of 1780—that is, we are "a government of laws, not of men." But many Federalists like Chase denied that such criticism of the government had a place in the republican scheme: He did not separate the institutions of government from the particular administration in power.[34] More than that, many Federalists doubted it was the place of an ordinary citizens to venture public criticism of the sitting government. The prosecutor reflected this mindset at the trial: "It is no less than to call into decision whether Thomas Cooper, the defendant, or the President of the United States, to whom this country has thought proper to confide its most important interests, is best qualified to judge whether the measures adopted by our government are calculated to preserve the peace and promote the happiness of America."[35] Cooper was in no place to second-guess the elected president of the United States. To do so was seditious libel punishable with imprisonment. The jury found Cooper guilty, and Chase fined him $400 and imprisoned him for six months for his criticism of Adams.

Despite Chase's insistence that elections mattered in republican government, James Callender was also prosecuted for his writings trying to influence the election of 1800. Callender, a Jeffersonian journalist who had come to American from Scotland, presented a choice between Adams and war and Jefferson and peace. He went on to call Adams a "hoary headed incendiary" who sought to "destroy every man who differs from his opinions." As if to prove Callender's point, Chase instructed the jury that, in protecting "our illustrious patriotic and beloved President," it was essential that those out of power yield their "private sentiments" once the government was elected. Chase piled on, insisting it was even worse that Callender's writings were done "avowedly for an electioneering purpose."[36] This left little room for political disagreement—even during an election year. Callender was found guilty, fined $200, and sentenced to nine months in prison. While Chase was intemperate in defending republican government against "licentious speech," even more sober and judicious Federalists shared his view of freedom of speech under the First Amendment.

Though he was not yet on the Supreme Court, the Great Chief Justice John Marshall argued that the Sedition Act did not "abridge" the liberty of speech and the press. Marshall's argument, like Iredell's and Chase's, depended on the common law understanding of seditious libel. The First Amendment did not alter this understanding. Indeed, Marshall thought this conclusion was easily drawn: Freedom of speech "signifies a liberty to publish, free from previous restraint, any thing and everything at the discretion of the printer only, but not the liberty of spreading with impunity false and scandalous slanders which may destroy the peace and mangle the reputation of an individual or of a community." A law punishing authors of "false, malicious and scandalous libels" is not an attack on "liberty of the press."[37] Turning to the text, Marshall noted that Congress is prohibited from making any law with regard to religion, but it "is only restrained from passing any law Abridging" the liberty of the press. The text was brought to life by way of historical understandings and the common law inheritance: Despite the change in the *form of government* from a monarchy to a republic, the meaning of free speech did not change.

Beyond the text of the First Amendment, Marshall appealed to the "necessary and proper" clause in Article I, Section 8, which gives Congress the power to "make all Laws which shall be necessary and proper for carrying into Execution the forgoing powers, and all other Powers vested by this Constitution into the Government of the United States, or in any Department of Officer thereof." Interestingly, Marshall objected to those—probably James Madison—who argued that the peculiar structure of "our government" never gave the Congress the power to regulate the freedom of speech. Marshall insisted that the First Amendment would never have protected speech if Congress could not reach it: "It would have been certainly unnecessary thus to have modified the legislative powers of Congress concerning the press, if the power itself does not exist."[38] Not only did the necessary and proper clause reach the issue, Marshall argued that even without the Sedition Act, libel against the government was punishable by a court. "The common or unwritten law which pervades all America, and which declaring libels against government to be punishable offence, applies itself to and protects any government which the will of the people may establish."[39] This was, for Marshall, an unwritten principle: The government must have the power to protect itself against libel and defamation in its own courts. And, in fact, several of the prosecutions for seditious libel under the Adams administration were done by way of the common law rather than the Sedition Act of 1798.[40]

Free Speech and Republican Government

Against this common law understanding of free speech, James Madison argued that the very idea of seditious libel was at odds with the American Constitution. It made no difference that the Sedition Act made truth a defense: Constructing the freedom of speech and the press in line with the common law inheritance was inappropriate for the kind of government the American people brought into being. Freedom of speech had a new meaning in America.[41] To understand this, we have to understand the foundations of the written Constitution and the revolution in government it reflected. Madison insisted that "it has been urged that the accused under the sedition act is allowed to prove the truth of the charge. This argument will not for a moment disguise the unconstitutionality of the act, if it be recollected that opinions as well as facts are made punishable, and that the truth of an opinion is not susceptible of proof. By subjecting the truth of opinion to regulation, fine, and imprisonment, to be inflicted by those who are of a different opinion, the free range of the human mind is injuriously restrained."[42]

Madison made this argument in helping pass the Virginia Resolutions in the state legislature, which were then published and sent to the other states and to Congress to persuade these bodies that the Sedition Act was unconstitutional and ought to be repealed. Madison further took to the newspapers to defend the Democratic-Republican Party in its fight against the Sedition Act and the Adams administration more generally, as well as defending the Virginia Resolutions in the "Virginia Report," written in 1800 and aimed at influencing the election. It was largely this report that Marshall was responding to in his defense of the Sedition Act. The arguments over the Sedition Act were part of the creation of political parties and the development of a distinction between the government and political parties, which would necessarily allow for what we now think of as the loyal opposition: parties that are loyal to the government itself and the constitutional scheme but disagree, often profoundly, with the party in power. To put this in perspective, consider that the election of 1800, when Adams stepped down from and Jefferson stepped into the presidency, is often thought of as the first peaceful transition of power between opposing political parties within a constitutional scheme.

Madison's argument largely turned on the nature of republican government and how the Constitution's text prohibiting the abridgment of freedom of speech and the press must be read in light of the nature and logic of republican government. Yet Madison began with constitutional text, quoting the First Amendment in full, which was still referred to as the Third Article of Amendment by both Madison and Marshall. Quoting it, Madison placed the key phrase in italics: "*or abridging the freedom of speech or of the press.*" The First Amendment was often still referred to as the Third Article of Amendment at the time because it was the third amendment in the list of twelve amendments Madison helped push through Congress in 1791, which then went to the states for ratification. The states ratified what we now call the Bill of Rights, the first ten amendments, in 1791, but did not ratify the first two at the time, which were still in play in 1798. (The second of the two amendments would later become the 27th Amendment to the Constitution, nearly 200 years later.) Notice that what we take to be a fixed, written Constitution clearly available to all citizens was in some flux in the first few decades of its existence. As the Yale Law School professor Akhil Amar reminds us, there was not always a readily agreed on text circulating among the people in these early years.[43]

Even so, there was little textual disagreement. Looking to the text, defenders of the Sedition Act argued that its meaning was "to be determined by the meaning of these terms in the common law."[44] Madison rejected this inheritance: "this idea of the freedom of the press can never be admitted to be the American idea of it." And this is because of the essential differences between the British constitution and the American Constitution. In the American system, power flows from the people, which requires a much more robust conception of freedom of speech, allowing the people—the popular sovereign—to criticize the government, which is bound by the Constitution. Leading Federalists' interpretations of the freedom of speech, which insulate the government from the people, were inconsistent with a republican government rooted in popular sovereignty.

This was a debate about first principles: What was the nature and logic of republican government? Underlying ideas about republican government would inform how we understood constitutional text. Public debate about the meaning of freedom of speech and the press during the ratification of the Constitution was largely indirect; it focused on the need to protect freedom of speech and the press by way of a bill of rights but rarely engaged the conceptual question of just what that protection would entail.[45] There was even less debate about the substantive meaning of freedom of speech in the framing and ratification of the First Amendment. Critics of the Constitution wanted alterations that would protect freedom of speech and the press, but what this looked like was not fleshed out. Most state constitutions protected freedom of speech and the press. Article XVI of the Massachusetts Constitution of 1780, authored by none other than John Adams, commanded: "The liberty of the press is essential to the security of freedom in a state: it ought not, therefore, to be restrained in this Commonwealth."[46] Many Federalists thought this perfectly compatible with punishing seditious libel that defamed the government. Contemporary practice was mixed. Blackstone's common law understanding had certainly been contested in America prior to the Revolution, and even in Britain it was not as uniform and fixed as Federalist defenders—and subsequent historians—made it out to be.[47] But neither was a robust understanding of free speech criticizing the government—and creating an opposition party to offer a clear alternative to the party in power—a fixed feature of free speech within America's new constitutional scheme.

Events forced political actors at the time to think through the meaning of freedom of speech: Textual meaning was constructed from the political theory that underlies the Constitution. Wendell Bird's extraordinary books on the history of the Sedition Act make clear how now forgotten figures—newspaper editors, political representatives, and ordinary folks who simply sought to speak their mind—helped forge a robust political understanding of free speech and press. Arguments against the Blackstonian understanding of freedom of speech and the press were part of creating a republican government rooted in individual rights and popular sovereignty—a government that provided for robust political dissent against the sitting government.[48] Madison might be understood as trying to create a political party that would embrace these understandings, constructing constitutional meaning based on "the sense attached to it by the people" that had been part of the development of these republican ideas over the last half of the eighteenth century.[49] Yet in the argument over freedom of speech, Madison might be better understood as teaching a deeply divided public how they must understand free speech, rather than drawing that understanding from the original public meaning. He engaged the public mind in an effort to shape it, to illustrate why constitutional text must accord with the broad construction of free speech. The

nature of governments elective, limited, and responsible, in all their branches, may well be supposed to require a greater freedom of animadversion than might be tolerated by the genius of such a government as that of Great Britain. In the latter, it is a maxim that the King, an hereditary, not a responsible magistrate, can do no wrong, and that the Legislature, which in two-thirds of its composition, is also hereditary, not responsible, can do what it pleases. In the United States the executive magistrates are not held to be infallible, nor the Legislatures to be omnipotent; and both elective, are both responsible. Is it not natural and necessary, under such different circumstances, that a different degree of freedom in the use of the press should be contemplated?[50]

Free Speech and the Centrality
of Differing Opinions

A republican government depended on citizens with the freedom to canvass "the merits and measures of public men." Not only would this require criticism of public officials and public policy, it also would allow criticism rooted in differing political opinions. To illustrate this,

Madison noted the First Amendment places freedom of religion alongside the freedom of speech. Freedom of religion protects different religious opinions in the same manner that freedom of speech protects different political opinions. For the very reasons that Iredell articulated at the North Carolina Ratifying Convention, Madison insisted that religious liberty under the American Constitution was altogether different from religious liberty in Britain. To interpret religious liberty in accord with the common law would frame constitutional text in line with pieces of the British political order that the American Revolution rejected. Yet this is precisely what defenders of seditious libel were doing with regard to speech.

According to Madison, this ought "to produce universal alarm; because it is levelled against that right of freely examining public characters and measures, and of free communication among the people thereon, which has ever been justly deemed the only effectual guardian of every other right."[51] We saw this with Justice Chase in the trials prosecuting Cooper and Callender. As these trials demonstrated, opinions and the inferences we draw from them cannot be subject to *proof* in a court of law. Or consider the case of Matthew Lyon, the first person to be prosecuted under the Sedition Act, which occurred before Madison's Virginia Resolutions. Lyon, a Democratic-Republican member of the House of Representatives from Vermont, criticized President Adams for "grasping at power," by way of the Alien and Sedition Acts (which Lyon had voted against as a member of Congress) and for taxing Americans to fund the quasi war with France. Lyon accused Adams of "an unbounded thirst for ridiculous pomp [and] foolish adulation."[52] Remind yourself that Adams thought the president should be called his majesty, his highness not being elevated enough. Adams even suggested, with no sense of irony, that the president be referred to as "The Protector of the United States' Liberties."

At his trial, Lyon defended himself, arguing that the act was unconstitutional because it criminalized his political opinions, but he also sought to demonstrate the *truth* of his opinions. He pointed to various acts of the Adams administration that suggested an effort to concentrate power—like the Sedition Act. The catch is that he could point to specific facts, but he reached conclusions based on those facts that were *political opinions*. Echoing Madison's argument, Lyon was attempting to bring Adams and his government into disrepute. He wanted to persuade his fellow citizens that Adams was not to be trusted with political power. In a phrase of remarkable foresight, Lyon insisted his expression of political opinions was "legitimate opposition" to Adams and the Federalists. Yet Lyon was found guilty of expressing "seditious opinions with bad intent." Justice William Paterson, who attended the Constitutional Convention and was appointed to the Supreme Court by George Washington, presided over Lyon's trial. Justice Patterson, like most of the justices who presided over Sedition Act prosecutions, did not let the jury consider facts but insisted that if Lyon expressed opinions with intent to harm Adams that was enough. Lyon was fined $1,000 and sentenced to four months in prison. The upside is he was re-elected from his jail cell and was released to a celebratory crowd.[53] He was charged again for his writings from jail against the Sedition Act, as well as for writings about his treatment at his first trial, which were central to his re-election campaign. Lyon's eluded prosecution.

But prosecution was widespread in an effort to silence opposition to the government.[54] Several figures were prosecuted for raising a "liberty pole" that included placards saying, "Liberty and Equality—Downfall to the Tyrants of America—Peace and Retirement to the President— Long Live the Vice-President and the Minority." Another was prosecuted for saying that Adams appointed "corrupt judges." One editor was prosecuted for gathering signatures to repeal the Alien Act. He was prosecuted a second time for publishing and criticizing a pending Senate bill on how to deal with disputed Electoral College votes as anti-republican. The bill was real but calling it anti-republican was sedition. The list goes on, but you get the picture. These prosecutions, and those to come like Cooper's and Callender's, confirmed Madison's fears that the Sedition Act allowed for the criminalization of political opinions.

In mattered not a whit that truth was a defense. Demonstrating the truth of political opinions, as if they were plain facts on which we could readily agree, was an impossible task against Federalist judges.[55] The administration's critics were not being prosecuted for "false statements of fact," as a later Supreme Court would put it. Nor were they being prosecuted for slander and libel as we now think of it; that is, telling willful falsehoods about public figures. These were not lies. This was not fake news. Lyon, Cooper, Callender, and numerous others were prosecuted because they pointed to generally agreed upon facts but deduced from those facts that President Adams was unfit for the presidency; his policies undermined republican government. There were no lies or falsehoods.

To be sure, political debate was not a polite affair in the early years of the republic. If you're distraught by our current political debate, a quick look at debate from the late eighteenth century suggests this is nothing new. Democratic-Republican papers called Adams a "liar" whose office was a "scene of profligacy and usury." He was dubbed a "hoary headed incendiary" whose "hands are reeking with the blood of the poor, friendless Connecticut sailor" and whose purpose was to "embroil this country in a war with France." This is strong stuff. It was meant to discredit President Adams. But is it true? How do we test this?

Despite the invective, there are claims about substantive issues here. The "poor, friendless Connecticut sailor" pointed to an active dispute about due process and foreign relations. At the center of the dispute was Jonathan Robbins, who claimed to be an American citizen from Connecticut. The British claimed he was Thomas Nash, an Irishman who committed crimes as a British sailor, and they wanted him turned over to them. Robbins/Nash was held in jail with no American charges and then turned over to Britain on Adams's order. Republicans thought Adams illegally and unconstitutionally slighted the rights of an American citizen, denying him due process by way of an executive power grab—all to curry favor with the British. Cooper even invoked judicial precedent under Washington at his trial to show Adams's disregard for the separation of powers.[56] Building on this, Democratic-Republicans thought that Adams was stubbornly set on war with France. They looked to France as an ally, not only for supporting the American Revolution in the past, but also in forging a republican government in the present. Despite the invective, there were serious constitutional and policy issues at stake.

The Federalist press engaged in similar invective. Federalist newspapers referred to Jeffersonian Republicans as "the refuse of nations" and "frog-eating, man-eating, blood drinking cannibals." Again, how do we determine if this is true? On some of it, we could try. There was probably little evidence of any Democratic-Republican being a blood-drinking cannibal. But were they the refuse of nations? Were they frog eating? Both refer to serious political questions. Federalists feared that Democratic-Republicans would allow unfit immigrants into the country with no regard to their background, education, or attachment to America's political principles. This was a debate about immigration and who should be able to become an American. Federalists also worried that Democratic-Republicans were allying with French Radicals—hence the "frog-eating"—and supporting a revolutionary movement that was devouring all who opposed it—perhaps the reference to "man-eating." To be an American was to support the government. Again, there are real issues at stake in this debate.

Yet, as we have seen, even sober and civil rhetoric could be subject to prosecution. In Congress, Jefferson's future secretary of the treasury, Albert Gallatin, argued that a concerned citizen who said the Sedition Act was a violation of the Constitution intended for partisan advantage rather than the public good could be subject to prosecution.[57] And indeed they were!

In a republican government, holding the government accountable requires information and debate that speaks to the "merits and demerits" of public officials and their policies. This means that all sides must be on an equal playing field. If the party in power can use governmental power to silence opponents, to criminalize differences of political opinion, the democratic processes itself is undermined. Public officials cannot be held to be infallible. Not even President George Washington. And, in fact, Benjamin Franklin's grandson took aim at Washington because his manners tended toward aristocracy, but, more crucially, the idea of government based on a great man was at odds with a republican polity and the rule of law. No government official should be beyond public reproach. Benjamin Franklin Bache was prosecuted for similar criticism of President Adams under the common law of seditious libel.[58]

The Sedition Act forced Americans to think carefully about the meaning of freedom of speech and the press under the new Constitution. Today we accept Madison's construction. Not because it was clearly vindicated by text, but because he brought out the essential characteristics of republic government that the written Constitution rested on.

***

These two early constructions of religious liberty and freedom of speech and the press reveal the necessity of turning to unwritten political principles and concepts to inform the written Constitution. The textual provisions that prohibited religious tests for office and that prohibited abridging the freedom of speech and press put forward commands rooted in political and philosophical principles. When Justice Chase spoke of vital principles of republican government, he was pointing to the ideas and theory that informed American constitution making. Chase, Iredell, Madison, and the other figures we've encountered in this chapter were all engaged in situating constitutional text within these unwritten understandings of the American constitutional enterprise. And their debates over constitutional meaning were debates about how to understand the political theory of America's republican government.

Whether we think of this as interpretation or construction, it is a process that requires us to draw out the logic of textual provisions by turning to more abstract understandings that are not encoded in constitutional text. While many of the examples in this chapter occurred outside the context of judicial interpretation, the same sort of endeavor is essential to judicial interpretation. The Supreme Court has not spent much time on Article VI's prohibitions of religious tests for public office, but the same sort of effort is evident in its interpretation of the First Amendment's prohibitions on laws "respecting an Establishment of religion, or prohibiting the free exercise thereof." How could it be otherwise? This clause (or clauses as it is usually understood) can hardly be understood apart from the political ideas and historical experience that informed the American understanding of religious liberty and separation of church and state. There are broad disagreements within this framework. Yet in examining the establishment and free exercise clauses, the Court looks to the history and ideas that inform these textual provisions. This includes the English political philosopher John Locke's *Letter Concerning Toleration* as well as the political and philosophic writings of James Madison, Thomas Jefferson, and others on church and state and religious liberty that helped inform the American approach.[59]

Text might be helpfully understood based on the history and debate that informed its framing and ratification. Yet when it comes to the First Amendment, whether it is religion or speech, understanding these more abstract provisions depends on the political theory that underlies the Constitution. Yet even plumbing these, we cannot escape making constitutional judgments of our own. If we take an originalist position to construct what a reasonable ratifier would have thought of these amendments, in the case of free speech its quite likely that there will be powerful evidence on both sides of the question (and that original meaning is underdetermined). As we've seen, this was precisely the case with Madison and Marshall with regard to freedom of speech and the press. Similarly, Chase and Madison disagreed on how to understand republican government in relation to seditious libel. Ultimately, we have to judge which understanding best comports with the principles and concepts underlying the American Constitution. We must construct meaning based on our best understandings of these principles and concepts.

This is inevitable. Even if the historical meaning of originalism were quite clear and even if it were fairly easy to construct what a reasonable person at the time would have thought about the First Amendment's application to speech and religion, we would still have to engage in some construction and judgment—what Lawrence Lessig dubs translation—about how to apply these understandings to contemporary issues. To contexts that were never conceived by those who framed and ratified the Constitution.[60] How does original meaning apply to corporations donating money to candidates for office?[61] Or what about for-profit corporations that seek religious exemptions from an otherwise valid law?[62]

However useful different versions of textualism and originalism might be in helping us think through such questions, we have to answer these questions for ourselves. Those worried about judicial overreach insist that the judiciary defer to the legislature where constitutional meaning is not obvious on its face.[63] Maybe this is best. But this, again, rests on a constructed understanding of the nature and logic of democracy that is not obvious from text. There is simply no getting around these judgments. And this is just as true when we turn to textual provisions that more clearly and concretely deal with institutional structure, as we will see in the next chapter.

4

Text and the Separation of Powers

Justice Antonin Scalia's lone dissent in the 1988 case of *Morrison v. Olson* is held as a model of textualism and originalism. So much so, despite that it was the lone dissent in a 7-1 Supreme Court opinion, and despite that the Court continues to follow *Morrison* as good law, Scalia's dissenting opinion is held to have been vindicated by most textualists and originalists in the three decades since he penned it. The Federalist Society hails it as "The Great Dissent."[1]

Morrison took up the constitutionality of the independent counsel, which is different than the special counsel you might have become familiar with during the presidency of Donald J. Trump. Like a special counsel, an independent counsel is appointed to investigate and, if need be, prosecute high-ranking government officials for violating federal law. The catch is, under the Ethics in Government Act of 1978, passed in the wake of the Watergate scandal, the independent counsel was appointed by a special division of the U.S. Court of Appeals for the District of Columbia. The independent counsel was thus appointed by members of the judiciary at the request of the attorney general based on a request from Congress. What's more, the attorney general could only remove the independent counsel for cause. The logic of the independent counsel was to insulate the office from immediate executive branch oversight. And this was because, as Watergate illustrated, problems could occur if the executive branch was tasked with investigating itself for possible legal wrongdoing. With the Ethics in Government Act, Congress sought to solve this problem by, first, authorizing members of the judiciary to appoint an independent counsel to investigate members of the executive branch at the request of the attorney general and, second, insulating the independent counsel from removal by the attorney general. Hence an *independent* counsel—as in independent from the executive branch. But is this consistent with the separation of powers?

The (Un)Written Constitution. George Thomas, Oxford University Press. © Oxford University Press 2021.
DOI: 10.1093/oso/9780197555972.003.0005

Theodore Olson, an assistant attorney general in the Office of Legal Counsel, insisted it wasn't. When the independent counsel investigating Olson for lying to Congress issued a subpoena to Olson for documents in the course of her investigation, Olson moved to quash the subpoena on the grounds that the independent counsel was unconstitutional. He found a sympathetic voice in Justice Scalia.

Executive Power and Text

Scalia had been on the Court for less than two years, but in *Morrison* he revealed the traits that would endear him to subsequent generations of textualists and originalists. Scalia's performance in *Morrison*, including during oral argument, pointed to the future. He rooted his argument in the logic of the separation of powers: The "principle of separation of powers is expressed in our Constitution in the first section of each of the first three Articles." Scalia then proceeded to a direct quotation of the first lines of the first three Articles to highlight the structure of the Constitution: "Article I, § 1, provides that '[a]ll legislative Powers herein granted shall be vested in a Congress of the United States, which shall consist of a Senate and House of Representatives.' Article III, § 1, provides that '[t]he judicial Power of the United States, shall be vested in one supreme Court, and in such inferior Courts as the Congress may from time to time ordain and establish.' And the provision at issue here, Art. II, § 1, cl. 1, provides that '[t]he executive Power shall be vested in a President of the United States of America.' "[2]

Here was the problem. The Constitution allocates a particular division of power among the branches of government, as is evident in constitutional text and structure, which illuminates the logic of separation of powers. As Scalia put it, "it is not for us to determine . . . how much of the purely executive powers of government must be within the full control of the President. The Constitution prescribes that they all are."[3] By situating an officer within the executive branch to exercise "executive" power, but placing them outside the president's immediate control, the Ethics in Government Act establishing the independent counsel violated the text of the Constitution, which requires that "all

purely executive power must be under the control of the President."
And the power exercised by the independent counsel appears to be
executive: "governmental investigation and prosecution of crimes is a
quintessentially executive function."[4] For Scalia, the very fact that the
independent counsel exercises some portion of the executive power
means that it must come under exclusive executive control; that is, as
an executive officer the independent consul must be subject to presidential control and removal. Yet the independent counsel was appointed by the judiciary and not subject to presidential removal. By
its very design, the Ethics in Government Act upset the constitutional
separation of powers: allowing the legislature to limit and control executive power that is constitutionally allocated to the president. Indeed,
Scalia insisted: "If to describe this case is not to decide it, the concept
of a government of separate and coordinate powers no longer has
meaning."[5]

If, at least, you accepted Justice Scalia's political theory of the separation of powers, which the Court did not. Chief Justice Rehnquist's
opinion for the Court spent most of its time parsing the meaning
of the appointments clause, Article II, Section 2, Clause 2, which
commands that the president "shall have the Power, by and with the
Advice and Consent of the Senate . . . to appoint . . . all other Officers of
the United States, whose Appointments are not herein otherwise provided for, and which shall be established by Law: but the Congress may
by Law vest the Appointment of such inferior Officers, as they think
proper, in the President alone, in the Courts of Law, or in the Heads
of Departments." To be somewhat simplistic about it, the Court held
that the independent counsel did not violate the appointments clause
because the independent counsel was an "inferior officer." And constitutional text gave Congress the power to vest the appointment of "inferior Officers" in "the Courts of Law" (or outside the president's reach).
Much as Scalia quoted the first lines of each of the first three articles as
dispositive, the Court pointed to the text of the appointments clause
as clearly demonstrating that Congress does have discretion to "determine whether it is 'proper' to vest the appointment of, for example, executive officials in the 'courts of Law.' "[6] Sorting out the appointments
clause, the Court then turned to how the independent counsel did not
violate the separation of powers.

Scalia insisted the Court had it backward. We must begin with the structure of government and the overarching logic of the separation of powers and situate the appointments clause within that context. Doing so, we can see that the Constitution's allocation of powers between the three branches would not allow the Congress to insulate an executive official from executive removal. End of the matter.

Yet for a textualist opinion, Scalia does not spend much time on text—beyond highlighting the allocation of powers. That's because the text itself does not describe the nature of executive power. And it's not so much that the Court in *Morrison* neglects the separation of powers, as that it does not agree with Justice Scalia's reading of "executive power" within the separation of powers. Scalia may be right, but his understanding of "executive power" is not clear from text. Nor, as we will see, is his originalist defense of it. Again, the crucial point is that his argument turns on an analysis of the "executive power" that depends on unwritten understandings. This was the source of his disagreement with the Court.

Executive Power and the Separation of Powers

Scalia's *Morrison* dissent begins with the famous statement from the Massachusetts Constitution of 1780 written by John Adams that we have "a government of laws, and not of men." The separation of powers seeks to secure this. Scalia then proceeds to quote James Madison's *Federalist* 47 to indicate that the framers of the Constitution understood the principle of the separation of powers to be essential to guarantee liberty under law. Having established the logic of a formal separation of powers, Scalia then insists that we should see constitutional text as reflecting this formal separation. But this interpretation depends on filling in the nature and logic of both the separation of powers and the executive power within that separation.

To fill in this logic, Scalia relies on the historical understanding of executive power and the political theory of the separation of powers that he sees underlying constitutional text. (Scalia's *Morrison* dissent, like many of his Court opinions, has little analysis of actual history or what would come to be called the original public meaning of text.) He argues that the powers the independent counsel exercises are executive in nature. We can identify these powers by what executives have traditionally done. And, as Scalia argues, "the powers at issue here have always and everywhere—if conducted by government at all—been conducted never by the legislature, never by the courts, and always by the executive."[7] There can be "no possible doubt" that the independent counsel's powers meet this description. Given this, they must be subject to executive control. Because the independent counsel is not subordinate to any "officer in the Executive Branch," the independent counsel cannot be regarded as an "inferior" officer under the appointments clause. The independent counsel must be subject to presidential control and removal as all "executive power must be under the control of the President."[8] We must read the appointments clause in light of these broader constitutional principles.

Yet these principles are disputed. On historical grounds, it has been argued that investigation and prosecution have not, in Scalia's words, always and everywhere been executive functions. In America, even during the framing and ratification of the Constitution, there was argument about this.[9] Perhaps more importantly, it is disputed whether the Constitution's separation of powers is as formalistic as Scalia makes it out to be.[10] Indeed, while Scalia cites Madison's *Federalist* 47 to make his case, it is worth noting that Madison raises questions in that very paper about being overly formalistic in our understanding. Like Scalia, Madison refers to the Massachusetts Constitution of 1780 and cites its command that in the "government of this Commonwealth, the legislative department shall never exercise the executive and judicial powers, or either of them." That document then goes on to pronounce this principle for each branch of government, concluding "to that end it may be a government of laws, and not of men." Interestingly, this was in the first section of the Constitution, which spoke to the declaration of rights, including general principles, and concluded right before the second part of the Constitution, which outlined the "frame of Government." Like many state constitutions from the period, the Massachusetts Constitution began by declaring rights and articulating *general principles*. The Constitution of 1787 does much less of this— there is the Preamble, which, with some irony, most textualists regard as out of bounds—yet we still depend on these general principles as Scalia's *Morrison* dissent reveals.

In fact, in *Federalist* 47, Madison cites the Massachusetts Constitution during the ratification debates to take on critics who insist that the new Constitution of 1787 does not maintain a *formal* separation of powers. Notice in the U.S. Constitution that the executive does exercise legislative power. The *president's* veto power is found in Article I, which as Scalia notes, deals with legislative power. Similarly, the *Senate* must confirm executive appointments and treaties under Article II, which as we've seen deals with the executive power. In *Federalist* 47, Madison defends these as part of checks and balances. In the course of doing so, he points out that the Massachusetts Constitution provides that "a number of the officers of government are annually appointed by the legislative department. As the appointment to offices, particularly executive offices, is in its nature an executive function, the compilers of the Constitution have, in this last point at least, violated the rule established by themselves."[11]

Let's be clear: Madison is praising this as a virtue. The Constitution he helped frame rejects this overly formalistic understanding as impractical as it requires that each branch be altogether sealed off from the other branches. In *Federalist* 37, Madison even noted that "no skill in the science of Government has yet been able to discriminate and define, with sufficient certainty, its three great provisions, the legislative, executive and judiciary." Questions "daily occur in the course of practice" about the nature and division of these powers that "puzzle the greatest adepts in political science." And that is because of the inherent limits of language—the very form of a written constitution—to convey complex ideas and concepts. Given the "complexity and novelty of the objects defined" some "inaccuracy" is unavoidable. Indeed, Madison went on to insist that when "the almighty himself condescends to address mankind in their own language, his meaning . . . is rendered dim and doubtful by the cloudy medium through which it is communicated."[12] Historically and philosophically speaking, the division between the different types of powers was not as stark as Scalia insisted but was prone to what Madison called "indistinctness." That's likely why, as Madison noted, that even while insisting on a general and formalistic separation of powers, the Massachusetts Constitution violated this principle in particulars. In *Federalist* 47, Madison labors to show that the general principle of the separation of powers must allow for some intermingling of powers between the branches to provide checks and balances, as well as for functional government. As Madison argues, the idea of separation of powers is violated only when "the whole power of one department is exercised by the same power which possesses the whole power of another department."[13] But that's hardly the case in *Morrison.*

Turning back to the text of the Constitution, we can agree that Article II, Section 1 grants "executive power" to the president, but does the text of the appointments clause allow Congress to limit and check executive power? May the Congress place the sort of limitations on the president at issue in *Morrison*? Scalia's argument rested on the idea that the executive must be democratically responsible. To be so, the executive must have complete control over the executive branch. Critics of Scalia's *Morrison* dissent highlight his misreading of executive power and point toward important checks on the executive. This argument depends on political theory, not simply on text. While Scalia argues that the president must be able to remove a subordinate officer in the executive branch, the Constitution's text does not actually specify executive removal under Article II. The text is silent on the issue. This was the first great constitutional debate in the First Congress when it sat in 1789.

Executive Removal and the Separation of Powers

The removal debate with its Decision of 1789, as the constitutional historian Jonathan Gienapp puts it, went to "the fundamental character of the Constitution itself."[14] Against the text's silence, three essential positions came out of the removal debate.[15] First, there were those who argued that impeachment was the only way to remove an appointed officer consistent with constitutional text: Article II, Section 4 concluded "the President, Vice President and all civil Officers of the United States, shall be removed from Office on Impeachment for, and Conviction of, Treason, Bribery, or other high Crimes and Misdemeanors." Second, others argued that because the Senate was required to appoint in the first place by way of Article II, Section 2, it was also necessary to remove an executive officer. Finally, there were those who argued that the executive alone ought to have the power to remove officers in the executive branch—even those officers who required Senate approval. This last position, which ultimately won out, had two variations. Some argued that the Constitution was silent on the issue, but that Congress in creating the departments of government could vest this power with the executive. Others argued that the Constitution itself vested the power to remove officers in the president as an inherent part of "the executive power." The debate is extensive and extraordinary, resulting from the creation of the secretary for foreign affairs. I urge you to have a look. If nothing else, you will almost certainly be heartened by members of Congress engaging in sophisticated constitutional debate. And keep in mind this was before the federal judiciary had been created by an act of Congress. Yet for my purposes, I simply want to highlight the various positions in relation to constitutional text.

Impeachment as the only way to remove an executive officer may seem extreme, but defenders like William Smith of South Carolina insisted that it was the only *textually* available process of removal. Smith's argument, to borrow from Justice Brett Kavanaugh, insisted on the "precise text of the Constitution." And he sounded remarkably like Justice Scalia in arguing that the various positions for executive removal "show us what ought to be, rather than what is, in the constitution."[16] He insisted if "the power be not found in the constitution, we ought not to grant it." If this is misguided or defective, the proper remedy is "to amend" the Constitution, but "as it now stands, we have no other way to remove an officer than by impeachment."[17] More than anything else, Smith and his allies worried that any other position "built" out from the Constitution was engaging in unwarranted "construction" that evaded the clear text of the Constitution.

Roger Sherman from Connecticut, a leading participant at the Constitutional Convention, was a powerful advocate for the position that the Senate was necessary to remove officers because it was necessary to appoint them in the first place. He also had text on his side: the appointments clause. As Sherman explained, "I think the concurrence of the Senate as necessary to appoint an officer as the nomination of the President; they are constituted as mutual checks, each having a negative upon the other." He continued: It is "an established principle, that the power which appoints can also remove, unless there are express exceptions made."[18] For instance, the text of the Constitution held that Article III judges held their offices "during good Behavior" so they were immune to removal *except* by impeachment. Similarly, the appointments clause allowed for alternative methods of appointment for "inferior Officers." If the framers of the Constitution had wanted the executive to be free to remove at will, the text of the Constitution could have clearly specified that, as it did in these other cases. If exceptions of this sort did not apply—and Sherman held they did not—then the Constitution commanded that Senate approval was necessary for removal.

Sherman got an assistant in this argument from William Smith, who turned to Publius's argument in *The Federalist Papers*, which insisted the Senate was necessary for removal just as it was necessary for appointment. Smith pointed to *Federalist 77*, the only paper to take up this question: "the consent of that body [the Senate] would be necessary to displace as well as to appoint."[19] He did so to reject Madison's argument that removal inhered in executive power as far too expansive a construction. What's more, Smith turned to the state constitutions to show that they did not follow this understanding of executive power. In this, Smith clearly gestured to arguments about original meaning in one form or another. Even more intriguingly, *Federalist 77* was written by Alexander Hamilton. And Hamilton is usually known for his expansive understanding of executive power and taken as the father of the unitary executive, which Scalia was putting forward in his *Morrison* dissent. Yet in *Federalist 77*, Hamilton argued that removal was not a necessary feature of executive power.[20]

Perhaps surprisingly, during the House debate it was Madison who argued that Article II's "vesting" clause necessarily gives the removal power to the president. Madison argued that the executive power granted to the president in Article II must include the power to remove all subordinates, not simply inferior officers, at his or her discretion. "It is evidently the intention of the constitution, that the first Magistrate should be responsible for the executive department; so far therefore as we do not make the officers who are to aid him in the duties of that department responsible to him, he is not responsible to his country."[21] For Madison, this was a debate that turned on the foundational character of the Constitution, and presidential removal was "most consonant with the *frame* of the Constitution."[22] Though he also insisted it was "most consonant with the text of the Constitution."

Madison drew this together by way of a "strict examination of the constitution, on what appears to be its true principles." In doing so, he turned to the opening lines of the first three articles, noting that Article I began by vesting all legislative powers "herein granted" in a Congress, Article II affirmed that the "executive power shall be vested in a President," and Article III declared that the "judicial power of the United States shall be vested in a Supreme Court, and in such Inferior Court as Congress may, from time to time, ordain and establish."[23] Given that the Constitution has separated powers into these great departments, we cannot qualify them any further than the Constitution does. So, for instance, Madison noted that the legislative powers are vested in Congress and cannot be exercised by another department, "except [where] the constitution has qualified it otherwise." The Constitution qualified the legislative power "by authorizing the President" to veto legislation. Yet the Congress retained "the absolute legislative" power with this qualification alone. Similarly, the Constitution "affirms that the executive power shall be vested in a President." Yes, Madison admits, there are also exceptions to this grant. The Senate, for example, must approve of presidential appointments. But the legislature cannot "diminish or modify" this executive authority. So the question is, "Is the power of displacing an executive power?" To this question, Madison gave a resolute yes: "if any power whatsoever is in its nature executive, it is the power of appointing, overseeing, and controlling those who execute the laws."

It was not enough to simply cite Article II's command that "the executive power" shall be vested in the president. This only raises the question, what is the "the executive power"? The text does not specify, so citing the text simply pushes us to construct the nature of the executive power. Madison offered a theory on the nature of the executive and why this was a logical understanding of it—even if the text did not clearly command this understanding. Madison began with the constitutional text but then turned to historical sources and conceptual analysis to draw out the logic of the separation of powers and situate the executive within that logic. Madison inferred the principle of the separation of powers—and the logic of executive power—from the text.[24] As Madison put it during the debates, if the president does not have the sole power of removal, "the President is no longer answerable for the conduct of the officer; all will depend on the Senate. You here destroy a real responsibility without obtaining even the shadow; for no gentlemen will pretend to say, the responsibility of the Senate can be of such a nature as to afford substantial security."[25] Having the Senate intrude on removal distorts the nature of executive power—the president cannot effectively carry out the duties of office if he or she cannot command those below him: "If the President should possess alone the power of removal from office, those who are employed in the execution of the law will be in their proper situation, and the chain of dependence be preserved; the lowest officers, the middle grade, and the highest will depend, as they ought, on the President, and the President on the community."[26]

Yes, there are checks on this power provided in the Constitution. But such checks need to be understood in line with the overarching nature of the separation of powers. A check on executive appointments limits executive power as Senate approval helps ensure the quality and character of public officers. Yet once placed in the executive branch, the executive needs to be able to control executive officers. Madison's analysis sought to explain why the text was silent on removal: In the context of the separation of powers, this power would obviously belong to the executive. Checks on this power, such as Senate approval, needed to be textually specified. Given this, Madison argued that we should interpret such limits narrowly.

More than the other arguments at issue in the removal debate, Madison drew out the deeper logic of the Constitution and the political theory it rested on. He argued that we must read text in light of unwritten principles. As Madison argued during the debate, "we ought always to consider the constitution with an eye to the principles upon which it was founded."[27] The debate was a preview of the sort of constitutional construction Madison would engage in nearly a decade later regarding the freedom of speech that I took up in the last chapter, showing why his reading of text was most consistent with the principles the Constitution brought into being. The term "construction" was used by all sides in this debate, which perhaps indicates that the text did not yield easy answers. Recalling the language of Federalist 37, Madison wrote in the midst of this debate that "the exposition of the Constitution is frequently a copious source."[28] While Madison hoped that Congress's construction would solidify and settle the matter by "precedent"—what he referred to elsewhere as "liquidation"—we've returned to these questions over the years.[29]

Even looking to the famed Removal Debate of 1789, it did not clearly settle the question. The executive was given the power of removal, but debate persisted over whether the Congress bestowed the power or whether the Constitution commanded it. As Gienapp argues, "Even though the Department of Foreign Affairs had been created, at the head of which would be a secretary, to be appointed by the president with the advice and consent of the Senate, and to be removed (if necessary) by the president alone, the question of exactly why the president had this power—the source of the surprisingly and prolonged debate—was as confused as ever."[30]

Translating Meaning?

Fast forward over 200-plus years of history to *Free Enterprise Fund v. Public Company Accounting Oversight Board* (2010), which raises familiar questions about the president's removal power. Without belaboring the details, in 2002 Congress passed the Sarbanes-Oxley Act to protect investors from fraudulent accounting practices from corporations. As part of a complex statutory scheme, it created the Public Accounting Oversight Board, which was under the supervision of the Securities and Exchange Commission (SEC). Members of the Oversight Board were removable by SEC for cause but not directly by the president. Did this violate the appointments clause or the removal power of the president? The Court found that it did, with Chief Justice John Roberts relying on the Decision of 1789. But just as I focused on Scalia's dissent in *Morrison*, I want to focus here on Justice Stephen Breyer's dissenting opinion. Both are careful about text and turn to history yet offer quite different understandings of executive power and removal.

Much like Scalia's dissent in *Morrison*, Breyer's dissent in *Free Enterprise* began with constitutional text and the separation of powers. Breyer noted, on the one hand, that the necessary and proper clause gives Congress "broad authority to 'create' governmental 'offices' and to structure those offices 'as it chooses.'" On the other hand, "the opening sections of Articles I, II, and III of the Constitution separately vest 'all legislative Powers' in Congress, the 'executive Power' in the President, and the 'judicial Power' in the Supreme Court." He thus agreed with Scalia's logic that these textual provisions point to "a structural separation-of-powers principle." Even more, Article II, Section 3's command that the president "shall take Care that the Laws be faithfully executed," limits Congress's power to structure governmental offices. Breyer recognized that certain executive branch officials, of the sort at issue in the Decision of 1789, must be removable at will.[31] Yet accepting these textual and structural principles, Breyer argued that this did not mean that the Constitution grants the president absolute authority to remove *any* executive branch official at will. On the contrary, depending on the nature of the office, Congress can constitutionally limit the president's power to remove certain officers. It depends, Breyer argued, on the nature of the office. Attending to constitutional text, he nevertheless insisted that we cannot look to more "specific constitutional text" because, beyond the vesting clause, appointments clause, and the take care clause, the Constitution is "silent with respect to the power of removal from office."[32] So we must engage in some construction on the question of presidential removal.

Like Scalia, Breyer also turns to history, though he finds the history more convoluted and vexed than Scalia did. While he agrees that the Removal Debate of 1789 is informative, particularly with regard to "principal" officers, it is much less helpful with regard to lesser officers. Breyer noted, for example, that the First Congress limited the "President's ability to oversee Executive Branch officials," pointing out that in 1789 Madison stated, "there may be strong reasons why an executive 'officer' . . . 'should not hold his office at the pleasure of the Executive branch' if one of his 'principal duties partakes strongly of the judicial character.'"[33] For Breyer, this suggested a much more functional understanding than Scalia's formal separation of powers. Drawing as much on text and history as Scalia did in *Morrison*, Breyer nevertheless argued that this conflict between two broadly framed constitutional principles could not be definitively answered by text and history. Given this, he insisted that we ought to interpret the text in line with a more functional understanding, as the Constitution was meant to create, by way of the separation of powers, "a workable government."[34] Doing so, he found that insulating a lesser officer from presidential removal was not an intrusion on "the executive power" or the president's ability to faithfully execute the laws. Indeed, Breyer argued, on separation-of-powers grounds rooted in text, this approach "embodies the intent of the framers."

Let us return briefly to Scalia's famed *Morrison* dissent. While it is much celebrated by textualists and originalists, it was also challenged on textualist and originalist grounds.[35] We can see these different interpretations as emphasizing different textual provisions of the Constitution in an effort to balance potentially competing institutional imperatives and constitutional principles. While Scalia highlights the centrality of executive power, others note textual limitations by way of the appointments clause and take care clause; there's also the fact that the text does not, as Scalia argues, actually say "all executive power" as opposed to "the executive power," which may be limited by other textual provisions.[36] Still, there's a powerful sentiment that Scalia's dissent was vindicated when Congress allowed the independent counsel statute to expire in 1999. Certainly, in the wake of Independent Counsel Kenneth Starr's investigation of President Clinton, which ended up focusing largely on Clinton's tawdry sexual relations with a young intern, there was a ready bipartisan consensus that the independent counsel's office had serious political and constitutional issues. In its place, the Department of Justice created regulations governing a more limited special counsel. In contrast to an *independent* counsel (appointed by three judges) the special counsel is appointed by the attorney general, the scope of the investigation is given by the attorney general, the special counsel reports on his or her findings to the attorney general, and the attorney general can remove the special counsel. This is the statute under which Special Counsel Robert Mueller was tasked with investigating Russian interference in the presidential election of

2016, including possible violations of law by President Trump and his associates.

Yet questions remain even for those who think the independent counsel went too far and that Scalia was essentially right in his *Morrison* dissent. Can Congress limit or constrain the president's ability to remove the special counsel to ensure a fair investigation? After all, if the president can remove the special counsel for any reason at all, he can effectively shut down an investigation into his own (possibly) criminal activity. What then? Even more, keep in mind that the Office of Legal Counsel in the Department of Justice—which is responsible for providing legal advice to the president and other executive agencies—says that a sitting president cannot be indicted *while* he or she is in office. Nothing in the Constitution says anything about this sort of immunity. Not a word. Every other officer in the government can be indicted. Why not a sitting president? Does this effectively place the president above the law?[37] How can we constitutionally limit the authority of those investigating the executive branch so that it does not become a witch hunt, while also providing for a genuine investigation? How should we deal with these competing constitutional imperatives? How do you ensure a fair investigation of the executive branch so that it is not the judge in its own case? If the president fires the special counsel to avoid findings of criminal activity, is that obstruction of justice? Can the president pardon himself? Are the only ways to hold the executive responsible for possible violations of the law and the Constitution by elections or impeachment? Can a president be impeached after he has left office?

You have to decide. Just as you will when it comes to the division of power between the executive and the legislature on issues of war and peace.

The Separation of Powers and the War Power

During the Korean War, President Harry Truman issued an executive order directing his secretary of commerce to seize and operate the nation's steel mills. For nearly two years, without any formal authorization from Congress, America had been fighting in Korea. Truman feared that a strike by the nation's steelworkers would halt the production of steel necessary to the war effort in Korea. Youngstown Sheet and Tube Company brought a suit, challenging President Truman's constitutional authority to seize its mills. Justice Hugo Black, writing for the Court's majority, found that President Truman overstepped his constitutional authority. Black began, not surprisingly, by noting that either the president's authority to seize the mills must come from an act of Congress or from the Constitution. Given that Congress had not authorized the president to take such action—and had in fact rejected such steps in recent legislation—Justice Black focused on the constitutional question.

The president's constitutional authority to take such action would have to come from Article II, Section I's vesting "the executive power" in the president; Article II, Section 2's command that the "President shall be Commander in Chief of the Army and Navy of the United States"; or Article II, Section 3's command that the president "shall take Care that the Laws be faithfully executed." Black quickly dismissed the argument that President Truman's power as commander in chief could reach a steel mill in Ohio given that the theater of war was in Korea. While Black entertained the idea that the theater of war in which the president could exercise his powers as commander in chief could be wide—and might even reach the domestic arena in certain cases—that was clearly not the case here. (Keep in mind that less than a decade before, Justice Black wrote for the Court in *Korematsu v. United States* [1944] upholding an executive order that placed Japanese Americans in "detention centers" because America was at war with Japan.) Black just as quickly dismissed the take care clause argument, insisting that there was no law the president was faithfully executing; it was, rather, a command from the executive branch.

So Truman's constitutional authority would have to stem from the president's "executive power" or some aggregation of inherent executive power. Yet Black spent very little time on the nature of "executive power," except to say "in the framework of our Constitution, the President's power to see that the laws are faithfully executed refutes the idea that he is to be a lawmaker. The Constitution limits his functions in the lawmaking process to recommending laws he thinks wise and vetoing laws he thinks bad. And the Constitution is neither silent nor equivocal about who shall make laws which the President is to execute. The first section of the first article says that 'All legislative Powers herein granted shall be vested in a Congress of the United States.' "[38]

Framing the seizure as a "legislative power," Black argued that allowing for such executive initiative inverts the role of the executive and the legislature. Justice Black's understanding of the separation of powers, and the power of the legislature and executive within that framework, placed the initiative for war and peace with the legislature. Executive power is, in many ways for Justice Black, about executing legislative initiative. Compared to Justice Scalia and others who dwell extensively on the nature of "executive power," Black is quite quick to see it in a limited manner. He certainly does not see any inherent executive power to protect and defend the nation. Nor did he see an inherent executive power allowing for the president to take the initiative in this regard. For Black, constitutional text makes clear that the "Founders of this Nation entrusted the lawmaking power to the Congress alone in both good and bad times."[39]

Black read constitutional text against the unwritten presumption of legislative supremacy and initiative. We saw a similar move in Black's understanding of rights in chapter 1: The legislature is presumed to have the power unless there is a textually enumerated right that limits it. Just as this reading is not textually required with regard to rights, it is not textually required with regard to legislative and executive power. Black embellishes constitutional text by presuming the sort of power being exercised is legislative in nature and therefore does not truly entertain the notion that Truman's exercise of power could be executive.[40] This was the argument of the dissenting opinion authored by Chief Justice Vinson: Under Black's view, "the President is left powerless at the very moment when the need for action may be most pressing and when no one, other than he, is immediately capable of action."[41] Following this logic against Justice Black, textualists like Scalia might say this is the very essence of "the executive power." Both readings are consistent with text, though both read text based on their underlying ideas about the nature of the separation of powers and the division of legislative and executive power within the constitutional scheme of war powers.

The Reach of Executive Power

In this vein, consider disputes over the nature and reach of executive power between Justices Antonin Scalia and Clarence Thomas— both of whom share an insistence on text and original meaning. In the 2004 case *Hamdi v. Rumsfeld*, the Court was asked to decide whether an American citizen picked up on the battlefield in Afghanistan could be labeled by the executive branch as an "enemy combatant" and indefinitely detained. President George W. Bush argued that during times of war, "the executive power" allowed the president to declare those who fight against the United States "enemy combatants" and deny them access to ordinary judicial proceedings—including American citizens. In an opinion by Justice Sandra Day O'Connor, the Supreme Court held that by authorizing the president to invade Afghanistan in the wake of September 11th, Congress had authorized the executive to detain "enemy combatants." Yet, the Court also held that Fifth Amendment due process rights allowed Hamdi to challenge his detention before a "neutral decisionmaker."[42] The Court argued that the executive branch had to provide some sort of forum in which those labeled "enemy combatants" could contest their status. And that forum had to be removed from the executive branch, though it did not have to be a judicial body.

Justices Scalia and Thomas markedly disagreed with the Supreme Court's opinion. But they did so for profoundly different reasons.

Justice Thomas agreed with the Court that Hamdi was not entitled to an Article III court's review of his enemy combatant status. Yet while the Court argued that the executive branch had to set up a process with a "neutral" review of its designation of enemy combatants, Justice Thomas held that it was entirely appropriate for the executive branch alone to make this determination. Thomas argued, "The Founders intended that the President have primary responsibility—along with the necessary power—to protect the national security and to conduct the Nation's foreign relations. They did so principally because the structural advantages of a unitary Executive are essential in these domains. 'Energy in the executive is a leading character in the definition of good government. It is essential to the protection of the community against foreign attacks.'" And the primary ingredient of "energy" Thomas argued, further quoting Alexander Hamilton in *Federalist* 70, was "unity." To this end Thomas insisted, "the Constitution vests in the President '[t]he executive Power,' Art. II, §1, provides that he 'shall be Commander in Chief of the' armed forces, §2, and places in him the power to recognize foreign governments, §3."[43]

Given that Hamdi was picked up in the battlefield of an active war authorized by Congress, Thomas argued that the judiciary was simply in no position to second-guess the executive branch's labeling Hamdi an enemy combatant. In separation of powers terms, this was beyond the capacity and competence of the judiciary. Because Congress had authorized the president to wage war in Afghanistan, it had also authorized the president to label and detain enemy combatants. In an active war authorized by Congress, the executive exercised the full extent of its powers conferred by Article II. Congress could plausibly place some limitations on these powers, but this was unnecessary to consider because Congress had authorized executive action; it was now up the executive how to proceed. It mattered not at all that Hamdi was an American citizen.

Justice Scalia disagreed. Turning from Article II of the Constitution and the conflict over executive power, Scalia insisted that when a citizen is accused of waging war against the government, as in Hamdi's case, the Constitution commands that he or she be prosecuted in court for a crime—including for treason, which is laid out clearly in Article III, Section 3, making plain it should be understood as a judicial proceeding with unique requirements. Barring prosecution for treason, the "Constitution's Suspension Clause, Art. I, §9, cl. 2, allows Congress to relax the usual protections temporarily."[44] That is, under Article I, Section 9, where limits are placed on Congress's powers, it is given a qualified exception with regard to the writ of habeas corpus. Under ordinary circumstances, due process requires that any person detained by the government be brought before a judge and formally charged with a crime. This allows the person to understand why they are being detained and it allows them to challenge their detention in court. Such ordinary procedures of detention and prosecution can be difficult in times of war. Given the exigencies of war, the Constitution allows Congress to suspend the writ of habeas corpus when in cases of "Rebellion or Invasion the public Safety may require it."

Yet absent a suspension of the writ of habeas corpus by Congress, Justice Scalia argued, the executive could not indefinitely detain a citizen. When the writ is suspended, however, "the Government is entirely free from judicial oversight."[45] But unless it is suspended, the Constitution commands that citizens cannot be indefinitely detained—they must be charged with a crime in an Article III court. While Justice Thomas's opinion turned to the history of executive power with a particular focus on the executive's ability to defend the nation, Justice Scalia's opinion looked to the history of habeas corpus and treason with a particular eye to the judicial protection of individual liberty against an overreaching executive. In doing so, they played up different textual provisions of the Constitution and situated those provisions in an overall understanding of the separation of powers and a weighing of constitutional imperatives.

A similar debate played out between these two justices with regard to the president's right to recognize a foreign nation. In *Zivotofsky v. Kerry* (2015), Manachem Zivotofsky's parents, in accordance with an act of Congress, requested that on his U.S. passport the State Department record his birthplace as "Jerusalem, Israel." The State Department, the executive agency responsible for issuing U.S. passports, did not officially recognize Israel's exclusive sovereignty over Jerusalem, so it declined the request and simply recorded Zivotofsky's birthplace as "Jerusalem." Zivotofsky's parents sued. Could an act of Congress require the executive to list Israel as the birthplace of American citizens born in Jerusalem if the parents requested it? Or did this impinge on executive power? Justice Anthony Kennedy, writing for a 6-3 majority, found that the act violated the president's power to recognize foreign nations and conduct foreign affairs under the Constitution.[46] But as in *Hamdi*, I'm interested in the dispute between justices Thomas and Scalia.

Justice Thomas began with the Constitution's allocation of powers over foreign affairs: "First, it expressly identifies certain foreign affairs powers and vests them in particular branches, either individually or jointly. Second, it vests the residual foreign affairs powers of the Federal Government—i.e., those not specifically enumerated in the Constitution—in the President by way of Article II's Vesting Clause."[47] Thomas held that the president had the right to regulate passports as part of "his residual foreign affairs powers." This is derived from vesting the executive power in the president, which includes the right to recognize foreign nations and conduct relations with them. The president thus appoints ambassadors, with the consent of the Senate, under Article II, Section 2. And under Article II, Section 3 receives ambassadors. But Thomas's essential argument relies on the nature of executive power in dealing with foreign relations. Congress cannot require the State Department, an office of the executive branch, to issue passports "recognizing" Jerusalem as part of Israel. To do so intrudes onto presidential power under the Constitution.

Thomas then took up Justice Scalia's argument that Congress, by way of the necessary and proper clause, can require the executive branch to list "Israel" on passports as part of bringing into effect its enumerated powers over naturalization. Article I, Section 8 gives Congress the power to "establish an uniform Rule of Naturalization." Thomas argued that this reading did not comport with constitutional text. The Constitution contained, he noted, "no Passport Clause, nor does it explicitly vest Congress with 'plenary authority over passports.'"[48] Noting that the government is one of enumerated powers, Justice Thomas argued that Congress may only act when it is authorized to do so. The necessary and proper clause is not enough in this case, because Congress's powers with regard to naturalization do not allow it to reach passports. Rather, the power to issue passports, done from the State Department, inheres in the executive power. This is why we see the power to appoint ambassadors to other nations, as well as the duty to receive ambassadors from other nations, in Article II. These are essential features of the executive branch. Allowing legislative intrusion into this area is not textually justified and cannot be a *proper* regulation under the necessary and proper clause because it is inconsistent with "principles of separation of powers."[49]

Justice Scalia accused Justice Thomas of creating "a presidency more reminiscent of George III than George Washington."[50] Scalia began with history, quoting William Blackstone on the king's royal prerogative, which included the "sole power of sending ambassadors to foreign states, and receiving them at home," as well as the sole authority "to make treaties" and the "sole prerogative of making war and peace."[51] The American people in their Constitution organized things differently: "the people therefore adopted a Constitution that divides responsibility for the Nation's foreign concerns between the legislative and executive departments." While the Constitution does give the president "the executive power," it qualifies some of that power by requiring legislative consent. Before turning to the president's power under Article II, Scalia establishes the statute's basis in congressional power under Article I. Congress's clearly enumerated power to make rules about naturalization enables it to grant American citizenship to someone born abroad. Given this, "the naturalization power also enables Congress to furnish the people it makes citizens with papers verifying their citizenship," including a passport. The necessary and proper clause confirms that Congress is enabled to make this power effectual. Yes, Scalia argues, Congress's powers have limits. Under the necessary and proper clause, legislation must not only be necessary for making an otherwise enumerated power effectual but must also be "proper." This law was both. It made effectual Congress's naturalization power and did not intrude upon the president's power to recognize foreign states. The executive retained the power to *not* recognize exclusive Israeli sovereignty over Jerusalem. Even if the "Constitution gives the President sole power to extend recognition, it does not give him sole power to make all decisions relating to foreign disputes over sovereignty."[52]

Indeed, Scalia argued that the Constitution clearly allows for shared authority in this area. Congress cannot force the president to recognize Israeli sovereignty over Jerusalem, but it can require that American citizens be allowed to list Israel as their birthplace when they happen to be born in Jerusalem. Scalia argued that Thomas's logic inverts the Constitution: "It turns the Constitution upside-down to suggest that in areas of shared authority, it is the executive policy that preempts the law, rather than the other way around. Congress *may* make laws necessary and proper for carrying into execution the President's powers, but the President *must* "take Care" that Congress's legislation "be faithfully executed."[53] This gives us George III exercising the royal prerogative rather than the constitutionally constrained presidency of George Washington.

Yet, much like their argument over executive power in the enemy combatant case, Thomas's and Scalia's arguments rest on an historically informed political theory of executive power, which underlies the separation of powers, and the kind of government the Constitution brought into being. Their argument, in fact, mirrors an early argument between Alexander Hamilton and James Madison on the nature of executive power.

A Republican Executive: Founding Quarrels

In 1793, with Europe in the midst of war, President Washington issued what would become known as the Proclamation of Neutrality, even though the term "neutrality" was not used. Washington's proclamation interpreted a treaty of friendship with France so that America would not be drawn into war on France's side. Yet the real disagreement regarded whether the Constitution granted the executive the authority to steer such a course. Hamilton defended Washington's authority as inherent in "the executive power." Madison, who as we saw made a powerful case for removal as rooted in the vesting clause, rejected Hamilton's logic regarding the proclamation of neutrality.

Hamilton wrote a total of seven essays as Pacificus in defense of the Proclamation of Neutrality, but it was the first essay that put forward the constitutional foundations of his argument. Hamilton grounded his argument in Article II's vesting clause: "The general doctrine then of our constitution is, that the EXECUTIVE POWER of the nation is vested in the President; subject only to the exceptions and qualifications which are expressed in the instrument."[54] The notion that the executive power is vested in the presidency, as we have seen, is but to quote the text of the Constitution. This may result in an extraordinarily powerful executive, or it may give us a limited executive, depending on precisely what is contained within the contours of "the executive power."[55] The clause itself, as you have already seen, does not answer this long-standing debate, but pushes us back to examine precisely what "the executive power" encompasses and how, then, exceptions to the power ought to be read.

Turning to the textual separation of powers, Hamilton began by asking what department of government was the proper one to make a declaration of neutrality. He quickly insisted that the legislature is "not the organ of intercourse between the US states and foreign Nations." Nor is the legislature charged with making or interpreting treaties or enforcing the obligations of treaties. He also quickly dismissed the idea that such a duty could devolve to the judiciary. The executive is both the organ of intercourse with other nations and the branch charged with executing the law—which includes treaties. Hamilton insisted this understanding was "natural and obvious" and so in tune with "general theory and practice" that we could only reject it if deductions from particular provisions of the Constitution contradicted it. Drawing on theory and history, Hamilton argued that the power to make treaties and the power to make war reside with the executive. But the Constitution made exceptions to this power. It required that the Senate ratify treaties and gave Congress the power "to declare war and grant letters of marque and reprisal." But these were "exceptions" to the executive power and ought to be read narrowly. In executing a treaty, the executive had the discretion to "preserve the peace."

Insofar as the Proclamation of Neutrality is an executive act, "the conclusion is, that the step, which has been taken by him [President Washington], is liable to no just exception on the score of authority."[56] And yet Hamilton did not deny what was textually obvious. The Constitution places the power to declare war in the hands of Congress: "the Legislature can alone declare war, can alone actually transfer the nation from a state of Peace to a state of War."[57] If history and political theory prior to the Constitution—particularly in British constitutional thought and practice—had rooted the power of making war in the executive, this power was given to the legislature in the American scheme.

Against his onetime co-author as Publius, Madison took up his pen as Helvidius to reject Hamilton's expansive definition of "executive power." Not surprisingly, Madison accepted Hamilton's textual readings. As we saw with the Removal Debate, the distinction between Article I's bestowing on the legislature "all power herein enumerated" on the one side, and Article II's granting "the executive power" to the president on the other—as well as Article III's granting the "judicial power" of the nation "to one Supreme Court and such other courts as shall be established"—was first expressed by Madison. While in the Removal Debate Madison argued that executive power must logically include the right to remove (significant) executive offers without Senate approval, in the debate over Washington's Proclamation of Neutrality he objected to Hamilton's expansive reading of the executive power.

Like Hamilton, Madison turned to history and theory to make sense of text. Although unlike Hamilton, Madison pointed to the novelty of America's republican scheme and how it broke with the British constitution and its tradition in important ways. He also argued that political thinkers like Locke and Montesquieu, while illuminating on the separation of powers, were still "clouded by royalism."[58] Madison, in particular, objected to Hamilton's inclusion of the treaty-making power and the war power within the scope of executive power. If the removal power was necessary for the executive to effectively execute the laws, this was far from the case with the treaty power or the war power. The treaty power, Madison argued, is itself the "force of a *law* to be carried into *execution*, like all *other laws*, by the *executive magistrate*."[59] Such a power cannot neatly fit within the definition of executive power. This is even more so with regard to the power to declare war. Constitutional text situates this power with Congress—and not as an exception, but as absolutely essential. As Madison argued, the power to move the nation to war is "one of the most deliberative acts that can be performed; and when performed, has the effect of *repealing* all the *laws* operating in a state of peace, so far as they are inconsistent with a state of war: and of *enacting* as a *rule for the executive*, a *new code* adapted to the relation between the society and its foreign enemy."[60]

The only real difference in textualist arguments between the former co-authors concerned the location of the treaty power. Given its location in Article II, which deals with the executive, Hamilton read it as an executive power that was limited, or checked, by way of Senate approval. Madison acknowledged the point but insisted we could not conclude from this that the power to make treaties was executive rather than "shared." Furthermore, he argued "when formed according to the constitutional mode" treaties are to have the "force and operation of laws, and are to be a rule for the courts in controversies between man and man, as much as any other law. They are even emphatically declared by the constitution to be 'the supreme law of the land.'"[61] As he had in constructing executive power in the Removal Debate and as he would with regard to freedom of speech, Madison's interpretation of constitutional text rested on the nature, logic, and theory of the new government the Constitution brought into being. It brought to life the unwritten—and deeply republican—understandings the text rests on.

***

Once more, you'll have to decide whether you think Hamilton or Madison is more persuasive, and how you think their arguments fit with the other arguments we've taken up by Scalia, Thomas, Breyer, and the like.

It's been suggested that the Constitution is an "invitation to struggle" with regard to the powers of war and peace. Certainly, these arguments have been with us since the beginning. And that's partly because much of the constitutional text is a variant of gray, rather than an exquisitely drawn distinction between black and white. Constitutional interpretation requires that we construct meaning around concepts like "executive power" that are not spelled out by text. The principle of separation of powers may begin in text—and often has very clear rules—but much of it has been constructed by way of political theory and historical experience. And, as these debates reveal, the text tends to be read in light of the reader's ideas and theories about the separation of powers. Beyond this, we are frequently called on to balance and weigh competing textual provisions. As we have seen in each one of these disputes about the separation of powers, the dispute is often over how to weigh and balance different, and perhaps competing, provisions of constitutional text, which may include competing constitutional values and principles. Our most pressing constitutional disputes rarely turn on discerning the meaning of a single discrete textual provision. On a range of issues, we must confront questions about how executive discretion fits with legislative lawmaking, the separation of powers, and the rights of citizens. And, as we've also seen, such questions continue to arise given new circumstances. We are engaged in a continual application of text and principle to new questions, weighing and balancing different pieces of text and different constitutional understandings, to fit them together as part of a constitutional whole.

5

Text and Unwritten Understandings

In the middle years of the twentieth century, a Michigan law required that all bartenders be licensed in cities with a population over 50,000. Yet it prohibited such licenses from being issued to women unless they were "the wife or daughter of the male owner." Valentine Goesaert, who owned a bar in Dearborn, a town with a population over 50,000 people, sued along with her daughter, arguing that the law violated the equal protection and due process clauses of the Fourteenth Amendment. Goesaert argued that she was discriminated against as a female owner and bartender. Unlike a male owner, she could not tend bar at her own establishment simply because she was a woman. And as a bartender, she could not tend bar because the owner was female rather than male. Her daughter joined the suit, noting that the law also treated the daughters of men differently than the daughters of women. If Goesaert were male, her daughter could tend the bar. But because she was a woman, her daughter could not tend bar.

Justice Felix Frankfurter, writing for a 6-3 majority in the 1948 case of *Goesaert v. Cleary*, was amused: "Beguiling as the subject is, it need not detain us long." Indeed, Frankfurter asserted: "To ask whether or not the Equal Protection of the Laws Clause of the Fourteenth Amendment barred Michigan from making the classification the State has made between wives and daughters of owners of liquor places and wives and daughters of nonowners, is one of those rare instances where to state the question is in effect to answer it."[1] Frankfurter was certain the Fourteenth Amendment's promise of equal protection of the laws did not prevent states from forbidding all women from working behind a bar. To be sure, Frankfurter noted, the law cannot "play favorites without rhyme or reason," but Michigan had reasonable grounds for its prohibition. The concern of drunken behavior, especially drunken men, was a clear justification to keep women from a situation they may not be able to control. If the legislature made exceptions for some

The (Un)Written Constitution. George Thomas, Oxford University Press. © Oxford University Press 2021.
DOI: 10.1093/oso/9780197555972.003.0006

women—wives and daughters of men—precisely because there would likely be a man nearby, that was all the more reasonable. Justice Black joined the opinion. He did not venture a word of justification, so we're left to fill in the reasons for ourselves. The question: Did Black join his frequent antagonist because of constitutional text? Or was it because he so readily accepted the unwritten assumptions of Frankfurter—who joked about Shakespeare's "alewife, sprightly and ribald"—with regard to gender? Put it this way, the text of the Constitution is clear: It requires that no person be deprived of the equal protection of the laws. But how do we determine when this has occurred?

The great antagonists Black and Frankfurter would join together a few years later in *Brown v. the Board of Education* (1954) to insist that race-based classifications were highly suspect and subject to the highest level of judicial scrutiny. The Court was unanimous in this position.[2] And Black had, in fact, laid the groundwork for this reasoning in one of the Court's ugliest moments, the Japanese "internment" case, where he found that racial classifications were invidious and could only be justified based on a narrowly tailored law to secure a compelling governmental interest.[3] But what of gender? Justice Wiley Rutledge, joined by two colleagues—brethren, as they were then called—insisted that while equal protection did not require "abstract symmetry" with "mathematical nicety," it did prohibit simple discrimination.[4] Justice Rutledge, like Frankfurter, was a law professor appointed by FDR. Also like Frankfurter, he agreed this was an easy case: Michigan was discriminating against women precisely because they were women. But we could similarly ask of Justice Rutledge, why does equal protection prohibit such discrimination?

The Centrality of Unwritten Understandings

We cannot answer this question without turning to history, principles, and theory. Textual provisions beyond equal protection don't give much help. Although it is interesting to note that not a single justice in *Goesaert* mentioned the Nineteenth Amendment, which guaranteed women the right to vote in 1920. Or to be textually accurate, prohibited the nation and states from denying women the right to vote "on account of sex." Might this suggest a standing for women that prohibits other forms of discrimination? Justice George Sutherland thought so. Noting the "diminishing intensity" in the inequality of the sexes, Sutherland argued that we had to account for the "great," indeed, "revolutionary . . . changes which have taken place . . . in the contractual, political and civil status of women" that culminated "in the Nineteenth Amendment."[5] Justice Oliver Wendell Holmes disagreed: "I will need more than the Nineteenth Amendment to convince me that there are no differences between men and women, or that legislation cannot take those differences into account."[6] Like his protégé Justice Frankfurter, Holmes argued that the judiciary ought to defer to the legislature, particularly in a case where it was making distinctions between men and women that were so obviously reasonable.

The catch is the dispute between Sutherland and Holmes was in 1923, which was 25 years before the Michigan case. Justice Sutherland wrote for the Court that Congress, in its legislative capacity for the District of Columbia, could not mandate a minimum wage for women but not for men. Sutherland argued that the distinction between men and women at the heart of the regulation was arbitrary. Like the Michigan law some two decades later, the justification might be to provide for the welfare of women, but as Sutherland saw it, the law is "confined to adult women (for we are not now considering the provisions relating to minors), who are legally as capable of contracting for themselves as men."[7] As a Senator from Utah, Sutherland had introduced the Anthony Amendment, named in honor of the great suffragist Susan B. Anthony, on the Senate floor. It would later take its place within the Constitution as the Nineteenth Amendment. Sutherland thought such changes made it clear, if it was not before, that women were entitled to equal treatment with men.[8] That may not preclude all distinctions on the basis of gender, but such distinctions could not be rooted in stereotypical assumptions about the "weaker sex," as women were referred to in briefs before the Court, to justify a minimum-wage law exclusively for women. And was this paternalistic tendency essentially the logic behind the Michigan law prohibiting women from being licensed bartenders unless a husband or father was presumed to be nearby?

Was Justice Sutherland basing his opinion on the evolving status of women in American society? Was this a kind of living constitution?

Was it an application of fixed principles to changing circumstances and understandings? Was deference to the legislature, displayed by both Holmes and Frankfurter, more consistent with constitutional text and the proper role of the judiciary?

The Role of the Judiciary as Constitutional Construction

Justice Sutherland is not usually associated with the idea of a living constitution. Far from it. As Sutherland wrote, "We frequently are told in more general words that the Constitution must be construed in the light of the present. If by that it is meant that the Constitution is made up of living words that apply to every new condition which they include, the statement is quite true." But, Sutherland continued, if by this we mean that the "words of the Constitution mean today what they did not mean when written" that robs the written Constitution of its very force. The judicial function is one "of interpretation" and does "not include the power of amendment under the guise of interpretation."[9] Following Sutherland, was he simply applying the constitutional text to new circumstances? If in the past we had not recognized women as men's equals, to do so now was not to change the Constitution but apply it to altered circumstances. Is this, essentially, the equivalent of applying the principle of freedom of the press to the internet? This seemed to be the crux of Sutherland's argument.

Justice Holmes, in contrast, is often identified as the most powerful proponent of a living constitution. But for Holmes, this usually meant judicial deference to the legislative branch in particular. It was the democratically elected branches—the legislature and executive—who could flexibly adapt the Constitution to altered circumstances. The judiciary, against the backdrop of majoritarian democracy, ought to restrain itself and defer to the democratic process. Indeed, in perhaps the most famous dissent in Supreme Court history, Holmes argued, "I think the word 'liberty,' in the 14th Amendment, is perverted when it is held to prevent the natural outcome of dominant opinion, unless it can be said that a rational and fair man necessarily would admit that the statute proposed would infringe fundamental principles as they have been understood by the traditions of our people and our law."[10] Holmes could be understood to say that the judiciary ought not to second-guess the legislature unless the case before it is obviously unreasonable; that is, we would have to say that the law in question *clearly* violates constitutional text or *clearly* violates fundamental principles as they have been understood by history and tradition. There *cannot* be a reasonable case on its side. Such laws are exceedingly rare.

On its face, Holmes's understanding of constitutional interpretation—and particularly the judicial role within the constitutional scheme—may seem much more modest than Sutherland's understanding. Certainly, Holmes expressed skepticism of reaching what he regarded as fraught judgments about principles or of reading into constitutional text. Yet Holmes's own understanding rests squarely on his view of democracy and the power of democratic majorities against unelected judges. It is a powerful judgment. Holmes writes eloquently of the "right of a majority to embody their opinions in law" and is rightly concerned with the prospects of judges reading their political predilections into the Constitution. We must take Holmes's case seriously. But doing so requires that we recognize that it depends on his conceptualization of democracy that underlies the Constitution. Whether it is the right understanding of American constitutional democracy or the one that best captures our constitutional project is at the center of this debate. But let's be clear that Holmes is engaged in such judgments about the political theory that underlie the Constitution. Turning the tables on Holmes, Justice Sutherland argued that judicial self-restraint "belongs in the domain of will and not of judgment." And that is because judges are called on to decide cases before them. In doing so, they should be bound by the Constitution as their oath requires. It is not for a judge to defer to democratically enacted legislation but to decide the case and overturn democratically enacted legislation if that's what the Constitution requires. Sutherland's stance rests on his understanding of American constitutional democracy and the role of the Court every bit as much as Holmes's does. Really, this is a debate about the institutional capacity of the judiciary. It is a debate, in Lawrence Lessig's terms, about both fidelity to the Constitution and fidelity to the judicial role.[11] Sutherland might be too cavalier in dismissing concerns about judicial lawmaking. He might also think that filling in the contours of constitutional text from his seat on the bench is easier than it actually is. Perhaps he is too quick to think that there are truly answers to all the questions that come before the Court. But, in a similar fashion, Justice Holmes's answer is to let any such questions be settled by, in his terms, a Darwinian democratic process.

Fixing the Constitution

Textualists hope to avoid such freighted questions by sticking to the text. Originalists hope to do so by sticking to the text as originally understood. But we cannot avoid the questions. This does not mean anything goes. Too often textualists and originalists argue that the only alternative to their approach is a freewheeling evolving or living Constitution. Yet this is misguided. The contrast between textualist originalism and living constitutionalism, important as it is to some issues, can be overdrawn.[12] Consider, again, Sutherland's opinion in the minimum wage case for women. Beginning with the text of the Constitution, Sutherland noted that the liberty protected by the due process clause of the Fifth Amendment—recall, this was a regulation of the federal government, so it's the Fifth Amendment in play, not the Fourteenth Amendment—included fundamental choices about work and labor within the terms of contract. He was quick to add that the government had a clear interest in regulating contract and labor conditions. The question, however, was why the law was regulating women in a way that it was not regulating men. For while the government may unquestionably regulate contracts, limiting the choices individuals can make, it cannot do so for arbitrary reasons. It may not treat similarly situated persons differently under due process of law.

Was there something different about women? Did the government have justification in treating women differently? Sutherland argued it did not:

> [W]e cannot accept the doctrine that women of mature age, *sui juris,* require or may be subjected to restrictions upon their liberty of contract which could not lawfully be imposed in the case of men

under similar circumstances. To do so would be to ignore all the implications to be drawn from the present day trend of legislation, as well as that of common thought and usage, by which woman is accorded emancipation from the old doctrine that she must be given special protection or be subjected to special restraint in her contractual and civil relationships.[13]

On the one hand, Sutherland is applying a principle derived, in his understanding, from the text of the Constitution. Yet there is no question that *changes in our social thinking* are responsible for just how that textual principle is applied in this case. There had been a change in the nation's thinking about the role and place of women.[14] Shortly after the passage of the Fourteenth Amendment, the Court found that the State of Illinois could prohibit women from becoming lawyers simply because they were women. Justice Joseph Bradley captured this logic, "the civil law, as well as nature herself, has always recognized a wide difference in the respective spheres and destinies of man and woman. Man is, or should be, woman's protector and defender. The natural and proper timidity and delicacy which belongs to the female sex evidently unfits it for many of the occupations of civil life."[15]

Sutherland was rejecting this understanding based on our altered ideas of what we now call gender differences. Sutherland acknowledged this important social, political, and civic change. Such changes were reflected in constitutional text by way of the Nineteenth Amendment. But the text of the Fifth Amendment and the text of the Fourteenth Amendment had not changed. Should the addition of the Nineteenth mean we apply the principles of the Fifth and the Fourteenth Amendments differently when it comes to issues dealing with gender? This is certainly one possibility. But it could also simply be that we apply the principle embraced in constitutional text to altered social circumstances—and these circumstances include a profound change in how society viewed women.[16]

To be sure, there had been long-standing agitation on this front. Not just from the framing and ratification of the Constitution, but more fully and powerfully from the Seneca Falls Declaration by Elizabeth Cady Stanton in 1848 to Susan B. Anthony's powerful textualist reading of the Fourteenth Amendment, "Constitutional Argument," published in 1872.

Anthony was arrested for voting illegally, because she was a woman, in Rochester, New York. Anthony argued that the Constitution prohibited discrimination against her. She turned to the text of the Constitution, arguing that the Preamble says, "we, the people, not we, the white male citizens, nor we, the male citizens; but we, the whole people who formed this Union." This included "women as well as men." If women were excluded from the terms of the people, if they could neither vote nor be voted in, they did not live in a democratic-republic, violating Article IV, Section 4 of the Constitution: "The United States shall guarantee to every State in the Union a republican form of government." Admittedly, these arguments required some philosophical abstraction about the nature of republican government and the people who created it. But they are essential to how we read constitutional text. And, let us ask, do they truly require more abstraction than the sort that originalism invokes?

Anthony was only getting warmed up. She noted that the Constitution did, on occasion, refer to "he, his, and him." For instance, Article II says "he shall hold his Office" referring to the president. Article II continues along these lines commanding, "Before he enter office" and "He shall have Power" and "He Shall from time to time." Article IV, Section 2 commands that a person charged with a crime in one state that flees to another be returned to the "State from which he fled." In these cases, Anthony argued, we read "he" in universal terms as a stand-in that also applies to women. If we do not read it that way, but see it as evidence to exclude women, this would also have to be true of laws in more general terms. All the laws that command "he, his, and him" do not apply to women, including the very law that Anthony was charged under. Yet Anthony's real point was that the "Fourteenth Amendment settled that question" because it insisted on the language of "persons." All persons born in the United States were citizens of the United States. And no person can be deprived of equal protection of the laws. The only question is, then, "Are women persons?"

Beginning with constitutional text, Anthony insisted: "Being a person, then, women are citizens, and no State has a right to make any

new law, or to enforce any old law, which shall abridge their privileges
or immunities. Hence, every discrimination against women in the
constitutions and laws of the several States is today null and void,
precisely as is every one against negroes."[17] Anthony's argument is a
brilliant reminder of the importance of constitutional interpretation by ordinary citizens. No doubt it was controversial at the time,
but it is consistent with text. Nearly a century later, Justice Ruth Bader
Ginsburg insisted on this point as a lawyer arguing against sex discrimination: Women had "full membership in the class 'persons' entitled
to due process guarantees of life and liberty and the equal protection of the laws."[18] In many ways, Anthony—and those who followed
like Justice Ginsburg—is more consistent with the actual text of the
Constitution than Frankfurter or Black or Scalia who are quite happy
to dismiss women's claims under the equal protection clause because
of history and tradition, not because of text.

Now Justice Black, as you might gather, returning to Sutherland's
argument about women, insisted that Sutherland had already de-
parted from constitutional text because he was protecting a liberty like
the right to contract. Sutherland was engaged, in this way, in reading
rights into the Constitution that were not textually there. Sutherland
was the poster child for the sort of jurisprudence Black wants us to
reject because it is the equivalent of moral philosophizing and judicial lawmaking. But Black's own theory of incorporation is not in the
text of the Constitution. I won't rehash the analysis from chapter 1,
just remind you that Black's incorporation argument engages in some
"substantive due process" of its own and is much less textually rooted
than he suggests. What's more, contract is, in fact, in the text of the
Constitution. Article I, Section 10 prohibits states from "impairing
the obligation of Contracts." More importantly, Black himself in his
Adamson dissent pointed us to the debates over the framing of the
Fourteenth Amendment. If we turn to these debates, we find "liberty
of contract" frequently mentioned. Some originalists suggest that the
precursor to the Fourteenth Amendment was the Civil Rights Act of
1866, which was an act of Congress to bring civil and political rights
to freedmen, erasing distinctions on the basis of race. It pointed to the
equal protection clause of the Fourteenth Amendment in demanding
equality and the privileges or immunities clause and the due process

clause in pointing to what rights should be protected. And the first liberty named in the Civil Rights Act of 1866 is the "right to make and enforce contracts."

This is a far cry from justifying Justice Sutherland's argument. Even if a right to contract is a privilege or immunity or citizenship or part of the liberty protected by the Fourteenth Amendment, there is still much to sketch in to arrive at Sutherland's defense of it as a general liberty secured by due process. And considering the context in which Sutherland wrote, it may be that even if liberty of contract is a constitutional right, how it is protected and regulated may well depend on context. That is, much as he seems to argue with regard to gender, a fixed constitutional principle may apply differently as social circumstances change. My only point is that Justice Black has as much work to do as Sutherland in filling in the logic and reasoning that underlie constitutional text to arrive at his conclusions about the role of the court in American democracy.

And what does Justice Black have to say to Susan B. Anthony? Whether it is textualism or the original understanding of text, we must again face the question: At what level of abstraction are we engaging? Here the distinction between so-called living constitutionalism and originalism may blur. Professor David Strauss of the University of Chicago Law School, a leading defender of the living constitution understood in common law terms, argues that the Constitution is built up over time from text based on evolving understandings like how we think about gender. Yet this is linked back with the "framers' genius" in leaving general provisions of the constitutional text general when need be. Such general provisions, rather than concrete and discrete textual clauses, are filled in and adapted over time.[19] Is this argument so different from originalists who would apply the fixed principles of the Fourteenth Amendment to gender discrimination even if the framers of the amendment didn't see these principles as applying to gender? The emphasis and tone may be different, but both of these positions might be captured by Justice Holmes's eloquent insistence that when we are dealing with the words of the Constitution, "we must realize that they have called into life a being the development of which could not have been foreseen completely by the most gifted of its begetters."[20]

The Inescapability of Theory

In the Michigan bartender case, don't we have to consider whether treating women differently than men denies them the equal protection of the laws? Doesn't the case invite us to reflect on the meaning of constitutional text as it applies to women? Don't we have to engage what the abstract command of equality requires? And won't social changes alter how we think about specific provisions? Even if we are only wanting, as the redoubtable Judge J. Harvie Wilkinson III urges, simply to decide cases based on commonsense legal understandings, we're going to engage in some level of abstract thinking. Justice Frankfurter was quick to say in this case that to ask the constitutional question is to answer it. Is that because he was all too willing to embrace stereotypical understandings of gender in 1948? Understandings, we ought to note, that three justices at the time thought unjustified. It's likely that if Justice Frankfurter were deciding the case in the early years of the twenty-first century, he would say much the same thing, but very likely decide the case the other way. Perhaps that's appropriate: The text of the law stays the same, but adjustments are made in our social and political understandings. Maybe it's best if the judiciary generally defers to such understandings.

This, certainly, is the logic of judicial restraint and judicial deference to our more democratic institutions. Nevertheless, the great justices imploring restraint like Justice Holmes and Justice Frankfurter could be labeled *theorists* of judicial self-restraint. And that is because their arguments for restraint rest on a deeper logic about the nature of American democracy and the role and capacity of the judiciary. In this sensible tradition, Judge Wilkinson urges us to remember the "first principle of our constitutional order." And that's the "inalienable right of self-governance."[21] Judge Wilkinson, like Holmes and Frankfurter, wants to persuade us against judicial overreach spurred on by "cosmic constitutional theory" from both the left and the right. But this modesty and restraint rests on a *theory of constitutional self-government* even if it is not fully theorized. Judge Wilkinson is right: We can avoid at times dizzying abstractions. But even a commonsense disposition to constitutional questions cannot avoid some level of abstraction and theory to make sense of constitutional text. Does it primarily protect constitutional self-government at the level of state governments? Does constitutional self-government require that all persons are treated equally as Anthony argued? Does it mean that all have an equal right to participate within the constitutional order? Does this include protecting rights like freedom of speech? Might it mean the judiciary has a particular role in protecting individuals in their rights and minorities against overreaching majorities to preserve self-government? Abraham Lincoln famously insisted that a notion of rights and equality was the basis of self-government.[22] Thomas Jefferson thought the judiciary might be uniquely situated to preserve constitutional self-government by protecting individual rights.[23] Perhaps more on point with the analysis here, the late Justice Ginsburg insisted over her brilliant career as a lawyer and jurist that constitutional self-government did not permit legislatures, made up overwhelming of men, to stigmatize women and treat them as second-class citizens.[24]

Judge Wilkinson and others who advocate for judicial modesty would almost certainly agree. Yet they would also engage in the refrain that against the Constitution's more abstract clauses, like due process and equal protection, we urge judicial modesty precisely because we are so uncertain. Why should judges fill out these abstract clauses, so to speak, rather than the democratic process? It's an excellent question. It nonetheless rests on a host of unwritten understandings about the nature and logic of the Constitution that are not so different from those who engage more readily in constitutional theorizing. In this sense, as Yale law professor Jack M. Balkin argues, translating abstract constitutional provision into their own context is "something judges actually do, whether they intend to or not."[25] As a practical matter, judges routinely engage in "interpretation-as-construction." This does not depend on a heroic understanding of the judiciary. And if defenses of a robust judicial role too often turn on an idealized version of judging, calls for judicial deference often turn on an idealized view of the democratic nature of legislatures.[26]

Originalists like Justice Scalia turn to original meaning to narrow the range of legitimate judicial interpretations of text. Confronted with the law the prohibited women from being bartenders, Justice Scalia would ask: What is the original understanding of the equal protection clause?

Asking such questions, we are already one step removed from text. It's not the general text that governs, but the original meaning of text. But in asking this, we are confronted almost immediately with a dilemma we've already seen: At what level of abstraction do we understand original meaning? As we saw in chapter 2, Scalia's answer is somewhat unclear. On the one hand, he insists on the most concrete understanding so as to confine judicial interpretation. This could be read as saying, if those who ratified the Fourteenth Amendment's equal protection clause did not think it applied to questions of gender, it does not apply to questions of gender. Certainly, then, there's no equal protection problem in discriminating against female bartenders. Or women more generally. On the other hand, at a more abstract level, Scalia rejects that he is a "time-dated" originalist; that is, original meaning is determined by the *expectations* of those who ratified the Constitution.

If this is the case, original meaning operates at a higher level of abstraction as we again saw in chapter 2. Did those who ratified the equal protection clause embrace a principle that it prohibited arbitrary classifications that could not be attached to a legitimate public purpose? Not only could such a principle reach female bartenders in Michigan in 1948, but it may also extend to same-sex couples in Michigan in 2015.[27] Defending the state's prohibition against same-sex marriage in *Obergefell v. Hodges* (2015), Michigan's Solicitor General John Bursch insisted that "the State of Michigan values the dignity and worth of every human being, no matter their orientation or how they choose to live their life. That's not what this case is about." The case, rather, was about preserving "traditional" marriage as it relates to procreation: "the marriage institution did not develop to deny dignity or to give second class status to anyone. It developed to serve purposes that, by their nature, arise from biology."[28] That is, marriage laws were developed to secure the flourishing of children, given the unique problems posed by heterosexual sex (it can result in children!).

Classifications between same-sex couples and opposite-sex couples were not, in this reading, arbitrary but attached to a legitimate public policy aimed at securing the welfare of children. Yet as the commonsense jurist Richard Posner pointed out in striking down state prohibitions on same-sex marriage, if laws governing marriage are about procreation, why allow couples who cannot procreate to get married? Even more, why make exceptions to laws in the case of first cousins, as many states do, precisely because the couples wishing to marry cannot procreate? If states are unwilling to apply the rationale invoked to prohibit homosexual marriage to heterosexual couples who cannot procreate, this might suggest the state was involved in an arbitrary classification violating either or both the equal protection clause and the due process clause of the Fourteenth Amendment. The question might then be: Do we think this sort of distinction is similar to distinctions on the basis of race that those who ratified the Fourteenth Amendment meant to prohibit? To be sure, this invites a more abstract originalism that may be too open-ended for some.

Certainly, it was for Justice Scalia. Dissenting in *Obergefell*, Scalia invoked self-government: "Today's decree says that my Ruler, and the Ruler of 320 million Americans coast-to-coast, is a majority of the nine lawyers on the Supreme Court." Scalia's turn to original meaning is worth quoting at length:

> When the Fourteenth Amendment was ratified in 1868, every State limited marriage to one man and one woman, and no one doubted the constitutionality of doing so. That resolves these cases. When it comes to determining the meaning of a vague constitutional provision—such as "due process of law" or "equal protection of the laws"—it is unquestionable that the People who ratified that provision did not understand it to prohibit a practice that remained both universal and uncontroversial in the years after ratification. We have no basis for striking down a practice that is not expressly prohibited by the Fourteenth Amendment's text, and that bears the endorsement of a long tradition of open, widespread, and unchallenged use dating back to the Amendment's ratification. Since there is no doubt whatever that the People never decided to prohibit the limitation of marriage to opposite-sex couples, the public debate over same-sex marriage must be allowed to continue.[29]

This is a powerful statement of original meaning: Constitutional text must be interpreted based on the specific understanding of those who ratified the amendment. And it links powerfully to Scalia's argument about self-government. The Constitution derives its legitimacy—and so binds future generations—precisely because it is an act of the sovereign people. As an act of We the People, the Fourteenth Amendment placed limitations on the states by way of granting rights to the people. The judiciary is obligated to protect the rights and limits bestowed by the sovereign people because it is a democratic act of a sovereign people that empowers the judiciary in the first place. Going beyond what We the People understood the amendment to be doing usurps our power of self-government and undermines the law.

Scalia is absolutely right, as a matter of history, that no one who ratified the Fourteenth Amendment in 1868 gave a thought to same-sex marriage. As he would have it, that resolves the case. Here Scalia seems to be giving a "time-dated" understanding of originalism. As Judge Wilkinson observes, "The original public understanding of a text is meaningless without also knowing at what level of generality that understanding took place."[30] The Fourteenth Amendment only protects the concrete expectations of those who ratified the amendment. Given that there is no historical evidence that any ratifiers thought about homosexuality at all, let alone same-sex marriage, the amendment simply does not have anything to say about the issue. Similarly, there is little evidence that those who ratified the Fourteenth Amendment thought much about sex or gender, so, following Scalia in *Obergefell*, it would not apply to discrimination on the basis of sex.

The Principle of Constitutional Self-Government

According to Scalia, states should make these decisions. This is part of the process of democratic self-government. As he has in numerous cases—particularly in cases dealing with sexual orientation—Scalia has insisted that the proper remedy for laws you don't like is to persuade your fellow citizens to alter such laws. That is the art of democratic self-government. But absent persuading your fellow citizens, democratic majorities have a right to make these decisions. Nothing in text as read through the lens of tradition has anything to say about sexual orientation. States are free to legislate however they choose in this area.

Justice Scalia's argument is partly rooted in the textualism we've seen: Only rights clearly enumerated in text or clearly protected by tradition are entitled to constitutional protection. Same-sex marriage does not count on this score. But Scalia's argument is also deeply rooted in his understanding of federalism and democracy. Under our federalist system of government, the states are the repositories of democratic self-government. While the national government is a government of enumerated powers, the states have wide sweep under their police powers to regulate the health, safety, welfare, and morals of the people. The states are only limited by way of Article I, Section 10, which limits specific actions on the part of the states—from passing ex post fact laws and bills of attainder to entering treaties or imposing tariffs. Article IV also requires that states grant the citizens of other states the same privileges and immunities of citizenship that they grant their own citizens. Various amendments also limit the states. We've seen this most vividly with regard to the Fourteenth Amendment, both in terms of equal protection and due process, but the Fifteenth, Nineteenth, Twenty-Fourth, and Twenty-Sixth Amendments limit states regarding voting rights. Other than these constitutional limitations, the states may prohibit abortion or allow it, provide for laws that protect against gender discrimination or not, provide for same-sex marriage or prohibit homosexual conduct simply because democratic majorities think it's immoral. They may do anything in between, including providing for civil unions, but not marriage. The beauty of democratically enacted legislation, unlike Supreme Court opinions, is that legislation can in fact go halfway and compromise.

Textual provisions point us to the importance of federalism; yet most of this understanding is part of the political theory that underlies the Constitution. What many jurists and scholars regard as the most important textual hook for federalism was added to the Constitution as the Tenth Amendment: "The powers not delegated to the United States by the Constitution, nor prohibited by it to the states, are reserved to the States respectively, or the people." This suggests that the national government is a government of enumerated powers, while the states retain all powers not enumerated. Notice the Tenth Amendment also says "or to the people" as an indication of popular sovereignty. The people retain that which they have not given up. We can also read this as the people exercising their power of self-government by way of the states. But whether the Tenth Amendment is a substantive limit on national power that commands a clear division between nation and states or simply a "truism" has been the subject of debate from the beginning. In *McCulloch v. Maryland* (1819), the Supreme Court upheld Congress's power to incorporate a national bank. The State of Maryland had objected, insisting that this was a power retained by the states because it was not a clearly enumerated power given to Congress under Article I, Section 8. Chief Justice John Marshall, in language we saw in the introduction, argued that the Constitution provided Congress a wide choice of means in pursuing its enumerated powers. Given the very nature of the written constitution, "only its great outlines should be marked, its important objects designated, and the minor ingredients which compose those objects, be deduced from the nature of the objects themselves."[31] According to Chief Justice Marshall, this was the idea entertained by the people themselves, and it was to be inferred from the nature of the written Constitution. Despite the State of Maryland's argument to the contrary, the Tenth Amendment did not alter this. It did not help that counsel for Maryland placed "expressly" before "delegated" in arguing before the Court, so the clause would read "all power not expressly delegated to the United States" is reserved to the states. This is what the Articles of Confederation had commanded, but the text of the Tenth Amendment dropped the word "expressly."

Still, debates about the delegation and division of powers between the nation and the states have continually arisen in our history. As Marshall put it, drawing this boundary depends on "a fair construction of the whole instrument."[32] And this depends not just on attending to different textual clauses but also on unwritten understandings to make sense of the whole. Scalia's reading gives wide latitude for self-government within the states, which are only bound by very clearly enumerated rights, while often limiting self-government at the national level by way of his understanding of federalism. Scalia, for example, insists on state sovereignty and "sovereign immunity" that limits national power.

In *Printz v. United States* (1997), Justice Scalia wrote for the Court striking down provisions of the Brady Handgun Violence Prevention

Act because they required state and local law enforcement officers to conduct background checks on prospective handgun purchasers. Scalia argued that the national government could not require state law enforcement officials to carry out federal policy—essentially commandeering the state governments for national purposes. Scalia drew on constitutional text and *The Federalist Papers* to insist that the states retained "a residuary and inviolable sovereignty."[33] Based on what Scalia called "essential postulates" inferred from constitutional text and structure, he insisted that conscripting state officials to carry out federal regulations violated the Constitution. Scalia's opinion yielded a robust understanding of federalism enforced by federal courts.[34]

Also drawing on constitutional text and *The Federalist Papers*, Justice John Paul Stevens insisted that Congress had ample power to act through state officials. He argued that historical materials suggested this was the understanding of the founding generation and quoted Alexander Hamilton from *Federalist* 27 to make the point that state and local officials may be "incorporated into the operations of the national government."[35] (Justice Souter piled on, quoting *Federalist* 36, 44, and 45 to the same effect.) Most importantly, whatever residue of state sovereignty might be found in the Constitution, Justice Stevens argued this was best protected by the national political process and not by the federal judiciary. Justice Stevens pointed out that the people of the states elected members of Congress. Even more importantly, constitutional structure gave each state two senators to ensure the state's voice in the national legislature: "it is quite unrealistic to assume that they will ignore the sovereignty concerns of their constituents."[36] Not only would federalism be better enforced by the political process than by way of federal courts, nothing in the text of the Constitution implicitly or explicitly forbids Congress from imposing "federal duties . . . on local officials."[37]

Neither of these understandings is obvious from the written Constitution. One understanding insists that the federal judiciary has a crucial role to play in drawing the boundaries between the states and the national government to preserve America's federal form of government. The other understanding insists that the Constitution does not offer such easy boundaries between national and state power for

the Court to draw on and that it's best regulated by the political process. This is an argument about where constitutional self-government
should occur, and what role the judiciary has in policing these
boundaries. It's an argument that's been with us from the beginning.

Constitutional Balancing

Whether it is prohibiting women from bartending, prohibiting same-
sex marriage, or requiring state officials to carry out federal policy, we
must decide how best to weigh and value potentially competing textual
provisions and constitutional principles. Doing so will inescapably
turn on our unwritten understandings, which might be best thought of
as constitutional constructions that situate discrete textual provisions.
That is, ideas about the implicit political theory of the Constitution
that are not themselves derived from text but guide our interpretation
of text, including how to prioritize competing provisions. Insisting on
judicial deference to the legislature because this best captures the logic
of constitutional self-government, for example, is its own constitutional construction. The insistence on constitutional self-government
pushes the question back, rather than answering it. What does it require? Does this mean the judiciary should take special care to protect the right to vote? Should the judiciary be particularly protective
of minority groups that might be marginalized by the democratic process? Should the judiciary ensure that "discrete and insular minorities"
are active participants in constitutional self-government? Should we
prefer constitutional self-government at the state level or the national
level when they conflict? Does this vary by constitutional issue?

All of these questions point to different features of constitutional
self-government that we must think through. There is a long-standing
strand of jurisprudence that situates the judiciary as most defensible
when it is protecting and reinforcing the democratic process.[38] The
idea is that in a democracy there is something inherently suspect about
unelected judges overturning democratically enacted legislation. So,
on the whole, the judiciary ought to defer to the legislative branch; it
should yield to the most democratic branch of government. As John
Hart Ely argues, the judiciary should only exercise the power of judicial

review when it is protecting the democratic process itself. The exercise of judicial review is most consistent with democratic self-government when it is used to ensure fair democratic procedures. This includes the right to vote and other rights, like freedom of speech, that are essential features of participating in democratic self-government. When the Court acts to protect the democratic process, it is not second-guessing democracy but reinforcing it.[39]

***

Yet we still must consider whether the judiciary should defer to state legislatures or Congress when the two conflict about democratic government itself. In a recent voting rights case, Justice Ginsburg argued that given the history of discriminatory voting procedures— particularly against blacks in many southern states—the Court ought to give wide latitude to Congress in order to protect minority voting rights. In doing so, she urged the Court to defer to Congress's information gathering and past record in eliminating race-based discrimination in voting, which had historically plagued America's democratic process. The Court, in an opinion by Chief Justice Roberts, argued that on the basis of "principles of federalism," the Congress should not require that certain states and counties get approval from the national government *before* enacting any law related to voting. True, there was a history of racial discrimination in these districts, but given that it was 50-plus years ago, the Congress should not treat states differently in this regard without a recent showing of discriminatory voting practices on the part of particular states. Chief Justice Roberts would defer to states and, in doing so, overturn sections of a congressional statute. Roberts took seriously the gravity of his decision, noting the Court should not overturn an act of Congress lightly. But it was unconstitutional, he argued, to subject certain jurisdictions to rules from the federal government without new evidence that these jurisdictions have engaged in racially discriminatory voting practices.

Like Justice Ginsburg's judgment, the chief justice's judgment was rooted in how he constructed relations among the states and national government, voting rights, and the Court's role in the constitutional scheme. Neither simply turned to constitutional text. Rather, based on

different textual provisions, an examination of history, and weighing
constitutional principles, they arrived at their judgments of what the
Constitution, taken as a whole, required. Most crucial to their respective judgments was the weight they gave certain constitutional
principles. Justice Ginsburg prioritized *voting rights* against a history
of racial discrimination, while Chief Justice Roberts prioritized *federalism* given the recent decline in racial discrimination in voting.[40]
These constitutional judgments, like all the others in this chapter, come
from constructions rooted in unwritten understandings and are the
real source of our debate.

Conclusion

The Inescapability of Constitutional Judgment

In the midst of the ratification debates, James Madison acknowledged the limits of the written Constitution he had done so much to shape.

> All new laws, though penned with the greatest technical skill, and passed on the fullest and most mature deliberation, are considered as more or less obscure and equivocal, until their meaning be liquidated and ascertained by a series of particular discussions and adjudications. Besides the obscurity arising from the complexity of objects, and the imperfection of the human faculties, the medium through which the conceptions of men are conveyed to each other adds a fresh embarrassment.

It was here, in Federalist 37 as we have already seen, that Madison insisted the "use of words is to express ideas. Perspicuity, therefore, requires not only that the ideas should be distinctly formed, but that they should be expressed by words distinctly and exclusively appropriate to them." And yet he then confessed "no language is so copious as to supply words and phrases for every complex idea, or so correct as to not include many equivocally denoting different ideas." From the beginning, Madison reminded us that "unavoidable inaccuracy" was an inherent feature of a written constitution.[1]

The (Un)Written Constitution takes constitutional text seriously. And yet, any attempt to make sense of the words of the Constitution necessarily rests on unwritten understandings of what the Constitution is and what it is meant to do. The interpretation of ideas and concepts denoted in text must come to terms with unwritten understandings. These background understandings determine how we interpret different provisions of the text and how we see them as part of a

The (Un)Written Constitution. George Thomas, Oxford University Press. © Oxford University Press 2021.
DOI: 10.1093/oso/9780197555972.003.0007

constitutional whole. The interpretation of the Constitution based on political theories must be acknowledged because these unwritten ideas drive our most persistent constitutional debates. As I hope this book has demonstrated, our recurrent constitutional debates are not between those who stick to the Constitution and those who abandon it for something else. Our constitutional debates are animated by what set of unwritten ideas and principles best capture being faithful to constitutional text. These long-standing debates are nothing less than an extended commentary on the political theory that underlies the American Constitution.

Whatever approach we take, we must make constitutional judgments—choices about underlying ideas and understandings—that are not answered by the text. To be sure, we should carry the burden of demonstrating why our understandings are consistent with the written Constitution; that is, why we think they make the best sense of the text. The text limits the range of plausible interpretations, but that does not relieve us of the responsibility to render constitutional judgments, rather it provides a common ground on which we all work.

Let us return to a question we began with: Is partisan gerrymandering unconstitutional? Is deliberately drawing the boundaries of a district to dilute the votes of one political party at odds with the Constitution? Recall, it was this question that moved Justice Gorsuch to ask if we can return to the "arcane matter, the Constitution." Justice Gorsuch was skeptical that the written Constitution provided standards that would allow the Court to decide such a question. In the language of the Court, is this question "justiciable"? Is it capable of being decided by courts? Or is it a political question? That is, a question that should be resolved by the political branches of government. As Chief Justice John Roberts put it, for the Court to remedy such problems there must be a legal right resolvable by legal principles.[2]

In the case of partisan gerrymanders, Chief Justice Roberts, while noting they were constitutionally problematic, concluded that the Constitution provided no clear standards for the Supreme Court to find them unconstitutional. Partisan gerrymanders are not forbidden by the Constitution—in fact, they have a long history in American dating back to the founding generation. The results of partisan gerrymandering seem unjust and incompatible with democratic principles, the chief justice conceded, but that does not "mean the so-lution lies with the federal judiciary."[3] The problem for Roberts was this: If it's acceptable for states in mapping electoral districts to take partisan interests into account, at what point do partisan interests be-come unconstitutional?[4] How much partisan gerrymandering is too much? The Constitution gives the Courts no guidance here.

This is a good lesson for us to learn. The Constitution is not a doc-ument for jurists alone. It depends on elected representatives and citi-zens to follow its text, spirit, and principles. Roberts is certainly right, many of the norms and principles we associate with our Constitution are not—and should not be—judicially enforceable. Hopefully, when citizens vote, they vote for candidates that embrace the idea that all people, regardless of religion or race, are equal citizens. Similarly, we hope that before taking office, when our representatives swear their oath under Article VI to uphold "this Constitution," that they've read the Constitution and have a sense of its structure, history, and princi-ples. Ditto for the president, who swears a unique oath under Article II before taking office to protect and defend the Constitution. Our republic depends on such commitments. But they are not judicially enforceable.

Pointing to the limits of judicial enforcement, Roberts conceded that in drawing districts within a state to create as many seats for one party as possible, the state legislature was almost certainly "diluting" the votes of individuals of the other party. But the Constitution does not embrace a proportional view of representation, commanding that each party is entitled to roughly as many seats in the House of Representatives as there are party voters in that state. Nothing in the Constitution requires that because Republicans make up 45 percent of a state's population that the Republican Party is entitled to roughly 45 percent of a state's seats in the House of Representatives. If it's ac-ceptable for the political party in power to give itself a slight advantage, nothing prohibits it from pushing its advantage as far as it can. For the Court to find otherwise, according to the chief justice, would be to import the Court's *substantive* understanding of democracy into the Constitution. The Court would be commanding a proportional system of representation when the Constitution does not. It's a problem of de-mocracy, but it's a political question to be solved by state legislatures, by Congress, and by the people themselves (including by constitutional amendment).

Yet let's be clear: The political questions doctrine is not commanded by constitutional text. It's a constitutional construction. And it was constructed by the judiciary.[5] That's not to say it's illegitimate. It is to say that the standards governing what constitutes a political question may not be so different than questions of what constitutes an unconstitutional partisan gerrymander. Roberts's opinion rests squarely on this construction created by the judiciary, which is based on its unwritten understandings of distinctions between law and politics.

Dissenting, Justice Elena Kagan pointed to textual provisions that gave the Court some guidance on this issue. She pointed to the equal protection clause of the Fourteenth Amendment and to the rights of free speech and association in the First Amendment. When states deliberately undertake to dilute or debase a citizen's vote, they are depriving that citizen of an equal chance to influence the political process. Even more, when they do so for deeply partisan reasons, they are diluting a citizen's vote precisely because of their political beliefs and opinions. Indeed, the state may be actively disfavoring certain political opinions in this case. The result of extreme partisan gerrymandering, when representatives pick voters rather than the other way around, is at odds with the idea that "power is in the people over the Government, and not in the Government over the people." At least so insisted Justice Kagan, quoting James Madison.[6]

Justice Kagan agreed with Chief Justice Roberts that judges should not impose their own ideas about "electoral fairness" on the Constitution. Nor should the Court find every whiff of partisanship problematic. The Constitution allows the states to come up with different public purposes in drawing their electoral districts. It does not command a proportional system of representation. Yet extreme partisan gerrymandering, where the *primary* goal in drawing boundaries is to make it more difficult for citizens of a certain political persuasion to achieve their goals via the democratic process, is at odds with both the Fourteenth Amendment's equal protection clause and the First Amendment's rights of speech and association. Justice Kagan accepted that states have different ways of drawing boundaries. Yet, drawing on past Court decisions, she offered a test for the Court that would allow it to prohibit extreme partisan gerrymanders: (1) The primary purpose in drawing boundaries was to entrench the party in power and dilute the votes of the other party, (2) the plan did in fact dilute these votes, and (3) there is no nonpartisan explanation for why the boundaries were drawn as they were. This test would allow the Court to apply a neutral standard in adjudicating claims of partisan gerrymandering rather than simply throwing up its hands in the face of a constitutionally distorted electoral process.[7]

To be sure, this was a judicially created test to enforce a constitutionally fair electoral process. It builds from constitutional text by constructing fundamental constitutional principles, and it then creates a judicial test to enforce them. Chief Justice Roberts's reliance on the "political questions" doctrine similarly relies on constructing fundamental principles from text and creating a judicial test to enforce these principles. Both jurists are ultimately making a constitutional judgment that relies on a constitutional construction that is not obviously commanded by constitutional text.

Creating standards that help guide the judiciary in resolving constitutional disputes is not particularly novel. Chief Justice Roberts did something quite similar in upholding the constitutionality of the individual mandate, as part of the Affordable Care Act (ACA), based on Congress's power to tax. The ACA required individuals to purchase health insurance or pay a penalty for noncompliance. The chief justice, along with four other justices, argued that the individual mandate could not be upheld as part of Congress's power to regulate interstate commerce. The question was whether the penalty could reasonably be conceived as a tax. The chief justice argued that it could. Yet in making this argument, he acknowledged that a tax could become so punitive that it was simply a penalty. At that point, it could no longer reasonably be conceived as a tax. Thus, while taxes can certainly be used to influence individual behavior—as they were in the ACA—there are limits to this power. Acknowledging these limits, Chief Justice Roberts nevertheless insisted: "we need not here decide the precise point at which an exaction becomes so punitive that the taxing power does not authorize it."[8]

In the ACA case, Roberts declined to answer his central question about partisan gerrymandering: How much is too much? Yet in both cases he made a constitutional judgment to guide his interpretation. Constitutional text says nothing about limits on taxes or taxes becoming so punitive they are unconstitutional, just as it says no such thing regarding partisan gerrymandering. In each case, the judiciary attempted to come up with rules and standards that allowed it to apply the written Constitution to the specific case before it. In both cases, the Court turned to unwritten constitutional understandings to make sense of the textual provisions at issues. All sorts of constitutional judgments must be made in doing so.

In arguing that the individual mandate was beyond the reach of Congress's power to regulate interstate commerce under Article I, Section 8, the chief justice insisted on a distinction between "inactivity" and "activity." He argued that Congress could regulate an individual's activity when they were engaged in interstate commerce. But being forced to enter the market when an individual was not active in it—that is, had not already purchased health insurance—was to force them into the market; it was to regulate "inactivity." The Congress, under its power to regulate interstate commerce, could no more force a person to purchase health insurance than it could force them to buy an automobile or broccoli in what was dubbed the "broccoli horrible." The text of the Constitution does not make any of these distinctions. Chief Justice Roberts made them, much as Justice Kagan made them regarding partisan gerrymandering, to best understand the meaning of Congress's power to regulate interstate commerce.

Chief Justice Roberts built on past Supreme Court opinions, which held that there must be things that are not part of interstate commerce—things that are beyond the reach of Congress's power—otherwise Congress could regulate any commercial activity it chose to regulate. In the past, in an effort to draw such boundaries, the Court had distinguished between "commerce" and "manufacturing" and between activity that had "direct" and "indirect" effects on interstate commerce. In opinions dating back to the late years of the nineteenth century, the Court had held that Congress could regulate commercial activity as part of its enumerated powers—but not manufacturing.[9] In this scenario, Congress could regulate goods that were traded between states (commerce), but it could not regulate the working conditions within the factories (manufacturing). In the early years of the twentieth century, the Court altered this standard, drawing a distinction between activity that had a direct effect on interstate commerce and activity that had an indirect effect. The Court held that the Congress under its commerce clause power could regulate activity that had a direct effect on interstate commerce, but it could not reach activity that had only an indirect effect on interstate commerce.[10] Roberts's distinction between activity and inactivity was part of a similar effort to construct the meaning of Congress's power to regulate interstate commerce: both to understand its scope and limits and offer the judiciary guidance in making constitutional judgments to enforce the limits of Congress's power.

Justice Ruth Bader Ginsburg insisted such "line-drawing exercises were untenable" and find "no home in the text of the Constitution."[11] Given the difficulty of drawing such boundaries, Ginsburg argued that in commerce clause cases the Court should presume the legislation is constitutional. Following this logic, she suggested that in commerce clause cases the limits of Congress's power are probably best enforced by way of "the democratic process" through elections rather than by way of legal constraints imposed by the Court. Ginsburg's argument drew on one of the most important constitutional constructions of the twentieth century: The idea that in most cases that come before the Court, the Court should presume the legislation to be constitutional. The exception to the presumption of constitutionality is legislation that interferes with the democratic process, touches on fundamental rights, or implicates a "suspect classification." When it comes to the democratic process, fundamental rights, or protected classifications, the Court should apply a more "exacting" level of judicial scrutiny, or what came to be called "strict scrutiny."[12]

Like the "political questions" doctrine, tiered judicial review was a construction to guide constitutional interpretation and offer standards for the judiciary to bring the Constitution to life. It rested on the idea that in most cases we ought to *presume* that the law is constitutional and let the political process play out. But it also acknowledged that if fundamental rights were at stake, the Court should be less willing to presume the constitutionality of a law. If citizens did not have the right to vote or speak out on political issues, we could not tell them to go to the polls rather than the courts if they did not approve of the law. In such cases, the judiciary has a special role in protecting rights, including the right to democratic self-government.[13] Along with self-government came the idea that certain rights were so essential to our conception of the American Constitution that they should be entitled to judicial protection. We have seen the different arguments, particularly in chapters 1 and 2, on how to identify what rights are "fundamental."

The point is that this, too, is a construction that builds from constitutional text and unwritten understandings. It is disputed. The "presumption of liberty" is thought by some to offer a better guide to constitutional interpretation than the "presumption of constitutionality."[14] It is an alternative construction. Some of these constructions are deeply influenced by originalist understandings and history. Others have been built up by judicial decisions as part of a common law constitutional understanding.[15] But textual readings we take for granted are often built up as part of an historical process and are not simple givens. Such constructions are a sort of political theory, guiding us to make sense of text, offering standards to shape our judgment in applying the written Constitution to particular cases. The propriety of these constructions, as we have seen with political questions and partisan gerrymandering, are deeply disputed. The idea that fundamental rights are subject to strict scrutiny was once deeply controversial. Recall the debates between Justices Black and Frankfurter from chapter 1. The Supreme Court came to accept this construction, even while the justices disagree over what counts as a fundamental right. Even originalist justices on the Court, as we saw in chapter 2 with Justice Scalia, accept the idea that fundamental rights are subject to strict scrutiny without attending to whether it is justified on originalist grounds.

The Necessity of Construction

Constitutional interpretation is frequently described as bringing out the latent meaning of text. The new originalism in particular holds that interpretation is a matter of bringing out the communicative content of text: How would an ordinary reader at the time a textual provision was ratified have understood the language of the text? This method draws on an analysis of dictionaries and usage from the time, often detached from the great political and historical controversies that surround the creation of such constitutional text.[16] This approach can be, as I've noted, illuminating when it comes to understanding particular words and phrases in the Constitution. An approach that complements the new originalism, corpus linguistics, where databases are searched to understand how language was used during a particular period, can also shed light on particular words or phrases in the Constitution. It could help us understand, for example, just what was meant by "emoluments" in Article I, Section 9 and Article II, Section 1.[17] This linguistic approach could help us gloss what the Second Amendment means when it uses "bear arms."[18] And some constitutional disputes turn on the specifics of language. What does the Constitution mean when it prohibits anyone holding a public office or trust from accepting an "emolument"? Yet when it comes to concepts like freedom of speech and religious liberty, separation of powers and federalism, the Stanford constitutional historian Jack Rakove reminds us that it is a *debate* we are interpreting.[19]

Consider the debate between Justices Scalia and Stevens on how to interpret the Second Amendment in *District of Columbia v. Heller* (2008).[20] How we understand "well-regulated militia" within the overall text was central to their disagreement about the Second Amendment and whether it provided an individual right to keep and own a handgun. But even here, where the discrete meaning of words and phrases was a crucial part of the disagreement, the disagreement still turned on historical and conceptual understandings. Justice Scalia analyzed the history of the right to bear arms to arrive at the conclusion that the operative clause of the Second Amendment, "the right of the people to keep and bear arms, shall not be infringed," was not subordinate to what he dubbed the prefatory clause, "a well-regulated militia, being necessary to the security of a free state." Justice Stevens rejected this ordering, insisting that the right to bear arms must be understood as part of a larger purpose of the amendment to secure state militias. If Justice Scalia was trying to focus on narrow textual meaning, Justice Stevens was focused on the purpose of the amendment.[21] But analysis of text alone cannot tell us which of these approaches to follow—especially if they happen to conflict. Even if we accept that interpretation should draw out the latent meaning of text, the text does not tell us how we should do so.

Leading originalists, as I noted in chapter 2, agree that originalist sources will "run out" with regard to clear meaning. When they do, we must turn to constitutional construction to "elaborate and supplement constitutional interpretation."[22] When this occurs, Randy Barnett argues, "the meaning of the text must be *determined* rather than found. After a level of generality is established historically, whether an object falls within or outside the ambit of a vague term is a matter of 'construction' rather than of interpretation. We could try to avoid such determinations of constructions by limiting the judicial application of constitutional terms to their core meanings, but such limitation would itself be a choice or construction and not the result of any interpretation."[23]

As we have seen, all interpreters are making constitutional judgments that are choices not determined by text and relying on constructions of one sort or another to do so. The separation of powers, federalism and dual sovereignty, judicial deference, and the like are all concepts that have been animated by constitutional constructions that are not clearly specified in constitutional text.[24] These principles and concepts form the political theory that underlies the Constitution and gives meaning to text. As Keith Whittington, a leading originalist argues, an approach that begins with "fundamental principles" or from the "structure or values implicit in or embedded in the constitutional scheme or language" may be "as useful as examining the constitutional text."[25] Others are skeptical that construction is truly different than interpretation. We might say that constructions are simply interpretations that turn to "fundamental principles" or "structure" or "values implicit in" the Constitution as part of the interpretive task. Whether we think construction is essentially the same as interpretation or something more, it is part of building constitutional meaning and applying constitutional text to the issues before us. This includes constructions that guide our understanding of text based on underlying concepts like the separation of powers and checks and balances, which can include the role and function of the different branches of government, the political questions doctrine, and the levels of judicial scrutiny. It also includes principles that underlie the text like due process of law and equal protection of the laws and ideas like freedom of speech and free exercise of religion.[26] Such constructions begin with constitutional text, but they must also turn to history, theory, and constitutional practice. All of this is part of understanding and ordering constitutional text and applying it in practice to a series of never-ending questions. Constitutional interpreters, including judges, are inescapably engaged in interpretation-as-construction— of applied political theory—when applying the Constitution to particular cases.[27]

We might say, as Judge Wilkinson does, that when textual materials run out, we defer to the democratic process. But, as I have had occasion to say multiple times now, this too depends on an unwritten background principle—the primacy of democracy—that is a constitutional construction. It, too, is akin to applied political theory. Why should this principle prevail against others? Is this what the Constitution commands? Should we weigh other background principles or understandings more heavily? Is it the structure of the Constitution? The presumption of natural rights? Of egalitarian principles? Of the democratic process? We must choose at some level; we must render these constitutional judgments. Answering these questions is essential to any interpretive effort and it requires some form of construction.

This is just as true for "pure" textualists who insist on the plain meaning of the text. In many cases, the plain meaning is fairly clear. Senators serve six-year terms, representatives serve two-year terms, and presidents serve four-year terms. Historically, we don't argue about these clauses because the plain meaning is clear. But what about Supreme Court justices who "shall hold their Offices during good Behavior." What constitutes good behavior? When can a justice be removed? What about impeaching a president for "high crimes and misdemeanors"? How does the impeachment process work? The text says that the House of Representatives shall have "the sole power of impeachment" and the Senate "the sole power to try all impeachments." Beyond specifying that when the president is tried the chief justice shall preside, the process remains open. The plain meaning of Article I, Sections 2 and 3, which speak to the impeachment process, does not say how this works or what constitutes high crimes and misdemeanors. Nor does it tell us if a president can be impeached after he leaves office.

This is an area where constitutional construction is specifically called for. As long as we follow the few textual rules—the House must impeach, the Senate try, and the chief justice preside if it's the president being tried—we can fill in the process in multiple ways. In this case, maybe the Constitution gives us discretion that is different from interpreting other clauses. Yet how to understand constitutional text when it comes to what constitutes high crimes and misdemeanors is precisely the thing we debate because the plain meaning of text is not clear—unlike how many senators each state gets. Where the Constitution commands that the Senate shall be composed of two senators from each state, we tend to take that as settled by plain meaning. When it comes to regulating interstate commerce or immigration, the powers of war and peace, or the division between nation and states, the meaning of freedom of speech and the press, the meaning of the establishment and free exercise clauses, we have much more to contest.[28] There is a lot of gray. Much of the constitutional text is clear only at the end of our process. Our interpretation of text will depend on how we read it in light of our unwritten understandings, principles, and commitments. Or, if you prefer, our antecedent understandings and political theory, those assumptions we make prior to reading the text, will shape how we read the text. These understandings structure our interpretation of text precisely because the answers are not obvious from the plain meaning of text itself.[29] A "pure" textualist is no different than others—they, too, must interpret the text based on some unwritten sources.[30] At the most foundational level, how we view the character and nature of the Constitution—what we imagine the Constitution to be—will shape our reading of its text.

Consider a recent originalist argument regarding the oath, which posits that the oath each public official takes in Article VI to uphold "this Constitution" necessarily refers to a constitution in accord with originalist understandings. The essence of the claim is that the referent to "this Constitution" must be to a fixed and time-bound constitution that does not change in its essentials and is understood based on the legal conventions when it was adopted.[31] This may be a persuasive argument, but it cannot plausibly turn on the text of "this Constitution" for that is precisely what is in dispute. How do we understand what "this Constitution" is? As we've seen, some defenders of originalism tend to collapse text and originalism—as if an originalist reading of the text is the obvious reading of the text because the Constitution is written and therefore the text equals an originalist understanding. Yet if we reject an originalist understanding of the Constitution, we can still insist on an obligation to adhere to "this Constitution." Indeed, it may be that we reject an originalist understanding of the Constitution precisely because we think such an understanding is *unfaithful* to the nature or character of "this Constitution." If so, originalists may be engaged in an act of constitutional creation, altering the Constitution by making it the sort of fixed object reducible to legal rules that they think it ought to be. The character and nature of the Constitution we are trying to be faithful to *is precisely what is being debated*. As the constitutional historian Jonathan Gienapp puts it, how we understand the Constitution is the central question before us: "This, it cannot be stressed enough, is the operative question. And there is nothing immediately helpful about answering, over and over: 'the text of the Constitution.' For this is less answer than dogmatic stipulation, one that tends to beg most important questions pertaining to the Constitution's core features and the character of its content."[32]

Being Explicit About Unwritten Assumptions

Unwritten ideas are part of every serious effort to faithfully interpret and follow constitutional text. The question is not, Is it legitimate to turn to unwritten sources beyond the written text? It's essential. The text cannot be the "sole legitimate source of operative norms in constitutional adjudication."[33] It does not speak for itself and cannot. The question is, What sources are legitimate to turn to? Do we bind ourselves to historical understanding? To original public meaning? Do we base our understanding on political principles and theory? On natural rights? On moral understandings and values? On ideals of justice? On some combination of these? Disagreement on these questions is the source of our recurrent constitutional debates—they are at the heart of how we understand fidelity to "this Constitution."

Consider again Justice Kavanaugh's insistence on the "precise text" of the Constitution. Paying attention to the precise text of the

Constitution will help us understand the structure of the Constitution. Most importantly, Justice Kavanaugh argues, it will help us understand the separation of powers. He notes something we have seen throughout this book, the first three articles of the Constitution point to the separation of powers. But what Kavanaugh wants us to understand is that the separation of powers is essential to protecting liberty—far more so than the Bill of Rights. And that is because the "separation of powers primarily protects freedom *from* government action."[34] The framers of the Constitution wanted it "to be hard to pass legislation." And they wanted it to be difficult to pass legislation because this would protect liberty. In making this argument, Kavanaugh notes the structure of the Constitution as reflected in text. He then turns to Madison and history to illuminate the text: The text is read through history, where the emphasis is on the political theory of checks and balances that allow the different branches of government to halt the actions of the other branches. This understanding of the separation of powers as an underlying constitutional principle is then used to understand constitutional text.

Yet Justice Kavanaugh, once again insisting on the precise text of the Constitution, spends very little time on it. Kavanaugh's argument is grounded in political theory and history. And rightly so. It's not clear that reading the precise text would lead to a complex understanding of the separation of powers and checks and balances. Kavanaugh's reading of text is a constitutional construction all the way down! It may be a powerful one, though other jurists and constitutional scholars would dispute his understanding of Madison—insisting that he has *confused* the concept of checks and balances with the concept of the separation of powers.[35] To say that Kavanaugh's argument rests on a constitutional construction far more than text is not a criticism. His drawing on text, historical sources, and political ideas from the founding generation illustrates how to construct underlying principles and concepts, which are then used to understand textual provisions.

Contrast Justice Kavanaugh to Ronald Dworkin, perhaps the most prominent defender of constitutional interpretation that commands a moral reading of the Constitution. Dworkin is frequently associated with moving beyond constitutional text to moral principles and, in Kavanaugh's terms, to making up new rights. Yet Dworkin, very much like textualists and originalists, firmly rejects the idea of a "living constitution" that evolves with the times. He insists that we cannot read our political or moral preferences into the Constitution. We must be faithful to constitutional text. Dworkin's formulation has strong affinities with certain versions of originalism. The catch, for Dworkin, is that he rejects the notion that the *original expectations* of constitutional text are the proper interpretation of that text.[36] Here he is following the dominant strand of originalism: Constitutional text itself—understood as what was enacted by those who framed and ratified the Constitution—is what we owe fidelity to and not to any particular *expectation* of how that text would be understood. As Dworkin puts it: "We are governed by what our lawmakers said—by the principles they laid down—not by any information we might have about how they themselves would have interpreted those principles or applied them to concrete cases."[37]

Dworkin distinguishes between the concepts the Constitution brought into being and the conceptions the framers and ratifiers had about those concepts. It is the former that make up the Constitution, not the latter. Dworkin goes even further in arguing that to understand constitutional text, to be faithful to the concepts put into existence by those who framed and ratified the Constitution, we must recognize "that they invoke moral principles about political decency and justice." Much like Kavanaugh's understanding of the separation of powers, Dworkin's moral principles underlie and animate the constitutional text. We cannot engage in good faith interpretation of constitutional text if we do not understand the moral principles that inform it. Not surprisingly, Dworkin's focus is on the Constitution's more abstract clauses—like the equal protection clause—that invite, as he puts it, broad readings. To read them more narrowly is to alter the constitutional text. To be faithful to constitutional text, particularly when it comes to more abstract clauses, requires us "to find the best conception of constitutional moral principles—the best understanding of what equal moral status for men and women really requires, for example—that fits the broad story of America's historical record."[38]

Dworkin may be wrong. Certainly, as the distinguished jurist and Stanford law professor Michael W. McConnell points out, Dworkin has an inordinate faith in judges. And he is quick to turn to abstract moral readings against more concrete historical understandings.[39] But Dworkin is not wrong because he has turned to unwritten understandings to inform constitutional interpretation. Here he is no different than Justice Kavanaugh. No different than Justice Black, Justice Scalia, or Judge Wilkinson. Dworkin situates judges as uniquely positioned to extract, or construct, constitutional meaning in such cases. He positions the Court as a "forum of principle": Independent judges, removed from the push and pull of politics, are most likely to interpret the Constitution disinterestedly, faithfully applying its moral principles to contemporary issues. From an alternative perspective, Judge Wilkinson pleads for judicial humility and modesty. Rather than have judges fill in the gray areas, courts ought to defer to the judgments of the democratically elected branches of government. The peoples' representatives are better positioned than unelected judges to fill in the gray areas.[40] In a democracy, we ought to insist on judicial humility. Dworkin may rely on an idealized version of the Court within the constitutional scheme, but this is no less true of Judge Wilkinson's idealized version of the legislature. Wherever you might come down, both these positions rest on unwritten understandings about the nature of American constitutional democracy. We cannot avoid this debate, whatever approach to constitutional interpretation we take.

***

These arguments are about the best understanding of constitutional text based on underlying concepts, principles, and values. How do we best construct our unwritten understandings based on text, structure, history, and constitutional development? How do we order different textual provisions along with our understanding of structure and principles? How do we weigh and balance potentially competing imperatives? How do we then understand these as part of a coherent constitutional whole and not simply as a jumble of discrete clauses? We cannot avoid making these constitutional judgments. The written constitution provides a framework in which we can think through the most persuasive understandings. We won't agree. But there's no avoiding the dispute and the judgments that come along with it.

Debates about how we draw these boundaries and balance these constitutional judgments has been with us since the framing and ratification of the Constitution. They are not going away. No one theory of constitutional interpretation is going to end them. Our written Constitution is simply not that clear. We are always going to have to make judgments about how best to apply the Constitution to our current circumstances and those judgments will always be subject to debate.

Welcome to the ongoing project of maintaining America's constitutional experiment.

Notes

Introduction

1. As Justice Gorsuch put it during oral argument, "When the Constitution authorizes the federal government to step in on state—state legislative matters, it's pretty clear. If you look at the Fifteenth Amendment, you look at the Nineteenth Amendment, the Twenty-Sixth Amendment, and even the Fourteenth Amendment, Section 2, says Congress has the power, when state legislators don't provide the right to vote equally, to dilute congressional representation. Aren't those all textual indications in the Constitution itself that maybe we ought to be cautious about stepping in here?" *Gill v. Whitford* (2018), oral argument, 59 at line 17, 60 at lines 1–9. https://www.oyez.org/cases/2017/16-1161.

2. *Gill v. Whitford*, oral argument, 59 at line at 17.

3. Neil Gorsuch, "Of Lions and Bears, Judges and Legislators, and the Legacy of Justice Scalia," 1 *Case Western Law Review* 909 (2016).

4. In Federalist 37, James Madison's insistence that words could not easily delineate and capture complex ideas was put forward in a discussion of the separation of powers. As Madison argued there, "Experience has instructed us that no skill in the science of government has yet been able to discriminate and define, with sufficient certainty, its three great provisions the legislative, executive, and judiciary; or even the privileges and powers of the different legislative branches." In Alexander Hamilton, James Madison, and John Jay, *The Federalist Papers* (New Haven, CT: Yale University Press, 2009), 182.

5. According to the constitutional historian Jonathan Gienapp, the very feature of *writtness* as central to understanding the Constitution was the subject of debate—indeed, it was ultimately part of an *evolution* in constitutional understandings. Gienapp, *The Second Creation: Fixing the American Constitution in the Founding Era* (Cambridge: Harvard University Press, 2018), 289. See also, Mary Sarah Bilder, *Madison's Hand: Revising the Constitutional Convention* (Cambridge: Harvard University Press, 2015), 5, 173.

6. On this trope, selling originalism as a way to make judges safe in a democracy, see Jamal Greene, "The Selling of Originalism," 97 *Georgetown Law Journal* 657 (2009).

7. Gienapp, *The Second Creation*, 23, 57.

8. Madison, Federalist 37, 183.

9. Keith E. Whittington, *Constitutional Interpretation: Textual Meaning, Original Intent, and Judicial Review* (Lawrence: University Press of Kansas, 1999), 13; Lawrence Lessig, *Fidelity and Constraint: How the Supreme Court Has Read the American Constitution* (New York: Oxford University Press, 2019), 69; and Jack M. Balkin *Living Originalism* (Cambridge, MA: Harvard University Press, 2013), 332.

10. Whittington, *Constitutional Interpretation*, 7.

11. Keith E. Whittington, "Originalism: A Critical Introduction," 82 *Fordham Law Review* 375 (2013).

12. Noah Feldman, "Trump and the Meaning of Impeachment," *New York Review of Books*, December 19, 2019.

13. Brett M. Kavanaugh, "Our Anchor for 225 Years and Counting: The Enduring Significance of the Precise Text of the Constitution," 89 *Notre Dame Law Review* 1916 (2014).

14. Alexander Hamilton, *Federalist* 78, 394.

15. *Marbury v. Madison*, 5 U.S. 137, 177 (1803).

16. *Marbury* at 178.

17. George Thomas, *The Madisonian Constitution* (Baltimore, MD: Johns Hopkins University Press, 2008), 29.

18. *Marbury* at 178–179.

19. David Robertson, *The Judge as Political Theorist: Contemporary Constitutional Review* (Princeton, NJ: Princeton University Press, 2010), 33.

20. Kavanaugh, "Our Anchor for 225 Years and Counting," 1923.

21. At the risk of being pedantic, in the constitutional text that is key to Marshall's finding the act of Congress before him unconstitutional, Marshall misquotes the constitutional text. Marshall found that Section 13 of the Judiciary Act of 1789 allowed the Supreme Court to hear some cases as cases of first impression—giving it original jurisdiction. Article III of the Constitution says, "In all other cases before mentioned, the Supreme Court shall have appellate jurisdiction, both as to law and fact, with such exceptions, and under such regulations as the Congress shall make." Yet Marshall put a period after "both as to law and fact." Note the Constitution places a comma, which then allows Congress to make exceptions, so that it might as a matter of statutory law move some kinds of cases from the

Court's appellate jurisdiction to its original jurisdiction. This is precisely what Section 13 of the act did. And it's most likely perfectly constitutional. It's odd that Kavanaugh, insisting on the precise text of the Constitution, does not note this. If we care about the precise text of the Constitution, we should understand that after the comma are exceptions that may seriously qualify the argument Marshall makes that brings the Constitution into conflict with Section 13 of the Judiciary Act. Look it up in your Constitution. Do as Justice Kavanaugh urges: Read *Marbury* along with the Constitution.

22. Akhil Reed Amar, *America's Unwritten Constitution: The Precedents and Principles We Live By* (New York: Basic Books, 2012), 5.

23. Griffith John McRee, ed., *Life and Correspondence of James Iredell* (New York: Appleton, 1857), 2:174.

24. James Madison to Thomas Ritchie, September 15, 1821. Madison wrote, "the legitimate meaning of the Instrument must be derived from the text itself; or if a key is to be sought elsewhere, it must be not in the opinions or intentions of the Body which planned and proposed the Constitution, but in the sense attached to it by the people in their respective State Conventions where it received all the authority which it possess." https://founders.archives.gov/documents/Madison/04-02-02-0321.   See   also, Jack N. Rakove, *Original Meanings: Politics and Ideas in the Making of the Constitution* (New York: Knopf, 1996), 339–42.

25. Eric J. Segall, *Originalism as Faith* (New York: Cambridge University Press, 2018) offers an insightful analysis of the various strands of originalism.

26. It may well be a half-baked or poorly thought through political theory, but as we will see, it's a theory all the same.

27. Rakove, *Original Meanings*, 10. See also, Bilder, *Madison's Hand*, 7.

28. Thomas Grey, "Do We Have an Unwritten Constitution?," 27 *Stanford Law Review* 703, 706 (1975).

29. Grey, "Do We Have an Unwritten Constitution?," 706, 709.

30. Ronald Dworkin, *Freedom's Law: The Moral Reading of the American Constitution* (Cambridge, MA: Harvard University Press, 1996), 10.

31. Greene, "The Selling of Originalism," 672.

32. Edward A. Purcell, Jr., *Antonin Scalia and American Constitutionalism: The Historical Significance of a Judicial Icon* (New York: Oxford University Press, 2020), 20.

33. *McCulloch v. Maryland,* 17 U.S. 316, 407 (1819).

34. Robertson, *The Judge as Political Theorist*, 8.

35. Ronald Dworkin, *Justice in Robes* (Cambridge, MA: Harvard University Press, 2006), 125.

36. Edward Corwin, *The "Higher Law" Background of American Constitutional Law* (Ithaca, NY: Cornell University Press, 1955).

37. Compare a leading originalist's testimony before the Senate on originalism with his scholarship. The scholarship acknowledges the importance of constitutional construction when the original meaning of the text is not clear. It's a key feature of the new originalism. Yet testifying before Congress, the emphasis was on how originalism constrains the judiciary and not a word was said about the necessity of constitutional construction. Lawrence B. Solum, "What Is Originalism? The Evolution of Contemporary Originalist Theory," in Grant Hustcroft and Bradley W. Miller, eds., *The Challenge of Originalism: Theories of Constitutional Interpretation* (New York: Cambridge University Press, 2011), 12–41; and Lawrence B. Solum, Statement of Lawrence B. Solum, Hearings on the Nomination of the Honorable Neil M. Gorsuch to be an Associate Justice of the Supreme Court of the United States, March 22, 2017, https://www.judiciary.senate.gov/imo/media/doc/03-23-17%20Solum%20Testimony.pdf.

Chapter 1

1. *Adamson v. California* 332 U.S. 46, 91 (1947) (Black, J., dissenting).

2. Hugo L. Black, "The Bill of Rights," 35 *N.Y.U. Law Review* 865, 869 (1960).

3. *Adamson* at 69.

4. *Adamson* at 71.

5. *Adamson* at 89.

6. *Baron v. Baltimore,* 32 U.S. 243 (1833).

7. Akhil Reed Amar, *The Bill of Rights: Creation and Reconstruction* (New Haven: Yale University Press, 1998), 213–214.

8. *Rochin v. California*, 342 U.S. 165, 172 (1952).

9. *Rochin* at 169 (Black, J., concurring).

10. *Rochin* at 167 (Black, J., concurring) and *Adamson* at 75 (Black, J., dissenting).

11. *Adamson* at 76 (Black, J., dissenting).

12. *Griswold v. Connecticut*, 381 U.S. 479, 510 (1965) (Black, J., dissenting).

13. *Griswold* at 522.

14. *Lochner v. New York*, 198 U.S. 45, 57 (1905).

15. *Jacobson v. Massachusetts* 197 U.S. 11, 25 (1905).

16. David E. Bernstein, *Rehabilitating Lochner: Defending Individual Rights Against Progressive Reform* (Chicago: University of Chicago Press, 2011), 38.

NOTES 153

17. *Meyer v. Nebraska*, 262 U.S. 390 (1923).
18. Randy E. Barnett, *Restoring the Lost Constitution: The Presumption of Liberty* (Princeton, NJ: Princeton University Press, 2004), 253.
19. Gary Jeffrey Jacobsohn, *Apple of Gold: Constitutionalism in Israel and the United States* (Princeton, NJ: Princeton University Press, 1993), 95.
20. Black, "The Bill of Rights," 870.
21. Barnett, *Restoring the Lost Constitution*, 138–139.
22. *Rochin* at 171. See Mark Silverstein, *Constitutional Faiths: Felix Frankfurter, Hugo Black, and the Process of Judicial Decision Making* (Ithaca, NY: Cornell University Press, 1984).
23. *Griswold* at 500–501 (Harlan, J., concurring).
24. *Griswold* at 500.
25. *Griswold* at 509 (Black, J., dissenting).
26. Charles Fairman, "Does the Fourteenth Amendment Incorporate the Bill of Rights? The Original Understanding," 2 *Stanford Law Review* 5 (1949) argued that the history around the framing and ratification of the Fourteenth Amendment clearly rejected the idea of incorporation in accord with Frankfurter's position. Subsequent scholarship, including originalist scholarship, has largely rejected Fairman's analysis while not entirely endorsing Black's position. Leading originalists debate whether the Fourteenth Amendment protects enumerated rights, for reasons somewhat different than Black put forward, or whether it protects enumerated rights plus unenumerated rights. See Kurt T. Lash, *The Fourteenth Amendment and the Privileges and Immunities of American Citizenship* (New York: Cambridge University Press, 2014), 94 (which argues essentially for an enumerated rights position); Amar, *The Bill of Rights*, 191, 200; and Barnett, *Restoring the Lost Constitution*, 53 (both of whom argue that the Fourteenth Amendment protects more than the rights enumerated in the Bill of Rights).
27. Barnett, *Restoring the Lost Constitution*, 224, 242.
28. *Griswold* at 510 (Black, J., dissenting).
29. Alexander Hamilton, Federalist 84, Alexander Hamilton, James Madison, and John Jay, *The Federalist Papers* (New Haven: Yale University Press, 2014), 435.
30. James Wilson, State House Speech, October 6, 1787 and Pennsylvania Ratifying Convention, Nov. 28 and Dec. 5, 1787, in Philip B. Kurland and Ralph Lerner, eds., *The Founders' Constitution* (Indianapolis, IN: Liberty Fund, 1987) 5:449, 453.
31. James Madison, Letter to Thomas Jefferson, October 17, 1788, in Kurland and Lerner, *The Founders' Constitution*, 1: 477–478.

32. *Griswold* at 525 (Black, J., dissenting).
33. James Iredell, North Carolina Ratifying Convention, July 28, 1788, in Kurland and Lerner, *The Founders' Constitution,* 1: 476.
34. *Corfield v. Coryell,* 6 Fed 546 (1823), 551–552.
35. *The Slaughter House Cases,* 83 U.S. 36 (1873). See Lash, *The Fourteenth Amendment and the Privileges and Immunities of American Citizenship,* 279, for an originalist argument that holds an enumerated-rights understanding of privileges and immunities, though for quite different reasons than Justice Black. Amar, *Bill of Rights,* 177–178, also rejects Black's understanding on originalist grounds.

Chapter 2

1. Antonin Scalia, "Originalism: The Lesser Evil," 57 *University of Cincinnati Law Review* 840, 863 (1988–1989).
2. Scalia, "Originalism: The Lesser Evil," 863.
3. Edward A. Purcell, Jr., *Antonin Scalia and American Constitutionalism: The Historical Significance of a Judicial Icon* (New York: Oxford University Press, 2020).
4. Randy E. Barnett, "Scalia's Infidelity: A Critique of Faint-Hearted Originalism," 75 *University of Cincinnati Law Review* 7 (2006). Other originalists, like Michael W. McConnell, have often been deeply critical of Scalia for not being a particularly faithful originalist. McConnell, "Free Exercise Revisionism and the Smith Decision," 57 *University of Chicago Law Review* 1109 (1990). Eric J. Segall, *Originalism as Faith* (New York: Cambridge University Press, 2018), 122–140, demonstrates Scalia's failure to draw on original meaning in much of his jurisprudence.
5. Akhil Reed Amar, "Introduction" to the new edition, Antonin Scalia, *A Matter of Interpretation* (Princeton, NJ: Princeton University Press, 2018), xviii.
6. Some leading liberal scholars consider themselves originalist. Akhil Reed Amar, *The Bill of Rights: Creation and Reconstruction* (New Haven, CT: Yale University Press, 1998); Jack M. Balkin, *Living Originalism* (Cambridge, MA: Harvard University Press, 2013); and Lawrence Lessig, *Fidelity and Constraint: How the Supreme Court Has Read the American Constitution* (New York: Oxford University Press, 2019). The Constitutional Accountability Center is a think tank and law firm dedicated to an originalist and progressive understanding of the Constitution (https://www.theusconstitution.org/about-cac/). And the

constitutional historian Jack N. Rakove situates himself within originalist understandings even while rejecting the notion that originalism is dispositive in interpreting the Constitution. Rakove, *Original Meanings: Politics and Ideas in the Making of the Constitution* (New York: Knopf, 1996), 8–9.

7. Steven G. Calabresi, a former law clerk, writes the afterword to the new addition of Scalia's *A Matter of Interpretation* released after Scalia's death. Ilan Wurman, a younger scholar, dedicates his book defending originalism to Justice Scalia. Wurman, *A Debt Against the Living: An Introduction to Originalism* (New York: Cambridge University Press, 2017).

8. Scalia, *A Matter of Interpretation*, 23.

9. Amanda Hollis-Brusky, *Ideas with Consequences: The Federalist Society and the Conservative Counterrevolution* (New York: Oxford University Press, 2019), xiii.

10. Jamal Greene, "The Selling of Originalism," 97 *Georgetown Law Journal* 657, 658 (2009).

11. Stephen E. Sachs, "Originalism Without Text," 127 *Yale Law Journal* 1 (2017).

12. Amy Coney Barrett, "Countering the Majoritarian Difficulty," 32 *Constitutional Commentary* 61, 81 (2017).

13. Scalia, "Originalism: The Lesser Evil," 854.

14. But see Larry Alexander, "Simple-Minded Originalism," in Grant Hustcroft and Bradley W. Miller, eds., *The Challenge of Originalism: Theories of Constitutional Interpretation* (New York: Cambridge University Press, 2011), 87–98, who defends original intent.

15. See, especially, Keith E. Whittington, *Constitutional Interpretation: Textual Meaning, Original Intent, and Judicial Review* (Lawrence: University Press of Kansas, 1999); Randy E. Barnett, *Restoring the Lost Constitution: The Presumption of Liberty* (Princeton, NJ: Princeton University Press, 2004); and Lawrence B. Solum, "What Is Originalism? The Evolution of Contemporary Originalist Theory," in Grant Hustcroft and Bradley W. Miller, eds., *The Challenge of Originalism: Theories of Constitutional Interpretation* (New York: Cambridge University Press, 2011), 12–41.

16. On original public meaning, see Randy E. Barnett, "The Gravitational Force of Originalism," 82 *Fordham Law Review* 411 (2013); and Lawrence B. Solum, "Originalism Versus Living Constitutionalism: The Conceptual Structure of the Great Debate," 113 *Northwestern Law Review* 1243 (2019). On original methods originalism, see John O. McGinnis and Michael B. Rappaport, *Originalism and the Good Constitution* (Cambridge, MA: Harvard University Press, 2013). For criticism of the new originalism,

Jack N. Rakove, "Joe the Ploughman Reads the Constitution, or, the Poverty of Public Meaning Originalism," 48 *San Diego Law Review* 575, 586 (2011); and Richard H. Fallon, Jr., *Law and Legitimacy in the Supreme Court* (Cambridge, MA: Harvard University Press, 2018), 61–67.

17. Jonathan Gienapp, "Constitutional Originalism and History," *Process: A blog for American history*, March 20, 2017, https://www.processhistory. org/originalism-history/. The constitutional historian Charles A. Lofgren, "The Original Understanding of Original Intent?," 5 *Constitutional Commentary* 77 (1988), illuminates the historical nature of the initial enterprise.

18. Calabersi, "Afterword" to new edition of Scalia's *A Matter of Interpretation*, 160–161.

19. *Planned Parenthood v. Casey*, 505 U.S. 833, 980 (1992) (Scalia, J., dissenting).

20. There is a question of whether Scalia accepts incorporation as a matter of originalism or precedent, Purcell, *Antonin Scalia and American Constitutionalism*, 107.

21. *Casey* at 1000. In contrast, see Barnett, *Restoring the Lost Constitution*, 224–252.

22. George Thomas, "Who's Afraid of Original Meaning?," *Policy Review* 164 (December 2010), 81.

23. Calabresi, "Afterword," in Scalia, *A Matter of Interpretation*, 151.

24. Calabresi himself argues that prohibitions on same-sex marriage violate the original understanding of the Fourteenth Amendment. Steven G. Calabresi and Hannah M. Begely, "Originalism and Same-Sex Marriage," 70 *University of Miami Law Review* 648 (2016).

25. *Lawrence v. Texas*, 539 U.S. 558, 592 (2003) (Scalia, J., dissenting).

26. *Lawrence* at 593.

27. *Lawrence* at 595.

28. *United States v. Windsor*, 570 U.S. 744, 801 (2013) (Scalia, J., dissenting).

29. *Michael H. v. Gerald D.*, 491 U.S. 110, 122 (1989).

30. Purcell, *Antonin Scalia and American Constitutionalism*, 101. For a critique of Scalia's textualism from a former president of the Supreme Court of Israel, see Aharon Barak, *Purposive Interpretation in Law* (Princeton, NJ: Princeton University Press, 2005), 29.

31. Thomas, "Who's Afraid of Original Meaning?," at 86–87.

32. Antonin Scalia, address, "The Common Christian Good," Gregorian University, Rome, May 2, 1996.

33. Purcell, *Antonin Scalia and American Constitutionalism*, 30. See especially Barnett, "Scalia's Infidelity," 13.

34. George Thomas, *The Madisonian Constitution* (Baltimore, MD: Johns Hopkins University Press, 2008), 140–142.

35. Jacob Howard, May 23, 1866, Congressional Globe, 39th Congress, 1st Session, 2766 (1866).

36. Kurt T. Lash, *The Fourteenth Amendment and the Privileges and Immunities of Citizenship* (New York: Cambridge University Press, 2014), 158.

37. See, from quite different originalist perspectives, Akhil Reed Amar, *The Bill of Rights: Creation and Reconstruction* (New Haven, CT: Yale University Press, 1998), 176–177 and Barnett, *Restoring the Lost Constitution*, 192–197.

38. Keith E. Whittington, "On Pluralism Within Originalism," in Grant Hustcroft and Bradley W. Miller, eds., *The Challenge of Originalism: Theories of Constitutional Interpretation* (New York: Cambridge University Press, 2011), 79.

39. Keith E. Whittington, "Originalism: A Critical Introduction," 82 *Fordham Law Review* 375, 379–382 (2013). See also, Solum, "What Is Originalism?," at 22–24. For a powerful critique of this turn, see Rakove, "Joe the Ploughman Reads the Constitution," 583.

40. See Gienapp, "Constitutional Originalism and History," for a lucid discussion of originalism 1.0 and 2.0. Though some originalist scholars— Michael McConnell and Kurt Lash, for example— turn largely to actual historical debates to draw out original public meaning.

41. Amy Coney Barrett and John Copeland Nagle, "Congressional Originalism," 19 *Journal of Constitutional Law* 1, 8 (2016).

42. Barnett, *Restoring the Lost Constitution*, 93.

43. Calabresi, "Afterword," in Scalia, *A Matter of Interpretation*, 154.

44. William Baude, "Is Originalism Our Law?," 115 *Columbia Law Review* 2349, 2380 (2015).

45. Michael W. McConnell, "Originalism and the Desegregation Decisions," 81 *Virginia Law Review* 947, 952 (1995). McConnell argues that there is historical evidence that those who participated in the debates thought it would require desegregating schools. McConnell's argument in this case illuminates the historical debates and draws out what those engaged in framing the amendment and other congressional acts at the time thought (a sort of framers' intent) to illuminate the best understanding of public meaning.

46. Barrett, "Countering the Majoritarian Difficulty," 61, 81. See also, Barrett and Nagle, "Congressional Originalism," 9.

47. James Madison to Henry Lee, June 25, 1824. Madison voices a version of what came to be dubbed original meaning with an emphasize on ratifiers

intent. "I entirely concur in the propriety of resorting to the sense in which the Constitution was accepted and ratified by the nation. In that sense alone it is the legitimate Constitution. And if that be not the guide in expounding it, there can be no security for a consistent and stable, more than for a faithful exercise of its powers." Madison even wrestled with the question of what level of generality we should focus on: "If the meaning of the text be sought in the changeable meaning of the words composing it, it is evident that the shape and attributes of the Government must partake of the changes to which the words and phrases of all living languages are constantly subject." https://founders.archives.gov/documents/Madison/04-03-02-0333

48. Segall, *Originalism as Faith*, 94–95.
49. Scalia, *A Matter of Interpretation*, 148–149. As Akhil Reed Amar says in the "Introduction" to the new edition, Scalia does not have a good answer to Dworkin, just vague generalities, xviii.
50. Michael J. Klarman, *From Jim Crow to Civil Rights: The Supreme Court and the Struggle for Racial Equality* (New York: Oxford University Press, 2004), 26, argues that *Brown v. the Board* is simply inconsistent with any grounded notion of originalism.
51. Scalia exercises no effort to make this originalist argument, either by drawing on history or by turning to textual and linguistic analysis. Scalia also rarely cites originalist scholarship on this question. The hard labor of originalism, despite the attention on Scalia, has been left to others. Jamal Greene points out that Scalia often does not turn to original meaning when engaged in questions of equal protection and due process, and that when he does, he often neglects the Fourteenth Amendment for the founding era. Greene, "The Age of Scalia," 130 *Harvard Law Review* 144, 157 (2016).
52. Scalia, *A Matter of Interpretation*, 149.
53. Scalia, *A Matter of Interpretation*, 149.
54. Segal, *Originalism as Faith*, 93.
55. Baude, "Is Originalism Our Law?," at 2381–2382.
56. In a statutory case, *Bostock v. Clayton County* 590 U.S. ___, 2 (2020) (slip opinion), Justice Gorsuch made a similar argument. Gorsuch insisted that "the limits of the drafters' imaginations supply no reason to ignore the law's demands." He went on to insist, "Only the written word is the law."
57. Purcell, *Antonin Scalia and American Constitutionalism*, 95.
58. *Kyllo v. United States*, 533 U.S. 27 (2001).
59. *District of Columbia v. Heller*, 554 U.S. 570 (2008).
60. Lessig, *Fidelity and Constraint*, 64.

61. Though even here there is a question of how original meaning—even if we can grasp it—is to be translated to our current context. As Lawrence Lessig puts it: "Translation gives us a clear way to understand two kinds of originalism—what I will call 'one-step originalism' and 'two-step originalism.' Translation itself is a two-step process. In the first step, the translator understands the text in its original context. In the second step, the translator then carries that first step meaning into the present or target context. This is two-step originalism." In Lessig's terms, Justice Scalia is a one-step originalist. Lessig, *Fidelity and Constraint*, 63–64.

62. Barnett, *Restoring the Lost Constitution*,120.

63. Keith E. Whittington, *Constitutional Construction: Divided Powers and Constitutional Meaning* (Cambridge, MA: Harvard University Press, 1999), 76; Whittington, *Constitutional Interpretation*, 5–12.

64. Barnett, *Restoring the Lost Constitution*, 122–123. See also Balkin, *Living Originalism*, 256–260.

65. Segall, *Originalism as Faith*, 89–102, offers a critical but helpful discussion.

66. Wurman, *A Debt Against the Living*, 86, and non-originalist, Fallon*, Law and Legitimacy in the Supreme Court*, 67–68. McGinnis and Rappaport, *Originalism and the Good Constitution*, reject construction as a legitimate feature of originalism.

Chapter 3

1. *Calder v. Bull* 3 U.S. 386, 388–389 (1798).

2. Whether these rights are principles of "natural" justice is a different question.

3. *Calder* at 388–389.

4. *Calder* at 388.

5. Jack M. Balkin, *Living Originalism* (Cambridge, MA: Harvard University Press, 2013), 256–257.

6. Antonin Scalia, *A Matter of Interpretation* (Princeton, NJ: Princeton University Press, 1989), 40.

7. *Calder* at 395.

8. Caldwell, North Carolina Ratifying Convention, July 30, 1788. Jonathan Elliot, *The Debates in the Several State Conventions of the Adoption of the Federal Constitution,* 4:199, https://oll.libertyfund.org/titles/elliot-the-debates-in-the-several-state-conventions-vol-4.

9. Iredell, North Carolina Ratifying Convention, July 30, 1788, 4:193.

10. Iredell, North Carolina Ratifying Convention, 4:194.

11. Iredell, North Carolina Ratifying Convention, 4:196.
12. Denise A. Spellberg, *Thomas Jefferson's Qur'an: Islam and the Founders* (New York: Vintage Books, 2013), 173–174, 178.
13. Iredell, North Carolina Ratifying Convention, 4:196.
14. George Washington, To the Hebrew Congregation in Newport, Rhode Island, August 18, 1790, Founders Online, https://founders.archives.gov/documents/Washington/05-06-02-0135.
15. Joseph Story, *Commentaries on the Constitution* (Durham: Carolina Academic Press, 1987), 700.
16. William Blackstone, *Commentaries on the Laws of England* (Chicago: University of Chicago Press, 1979), 4:53.
17. Terri Diane Halperin, *The Alien and Sedition Acts of 1798* (Baltimore, MD: Johns Hopkins University Press, 2018), 54, 56.
18. Halperin, *The Alien and Sedition Acts*, 29.
19. Jud Campbell, "Natural Rights and the First Amendment," 127 *Yale Law Journal* 246 (2017), notes the various understandings of different rights related to speech and press during this period.
20. Wendell Bird, *The Revolution in Freedoms of Press and Speech: From Blackstone to the First Amendment and Fox's Libel Act* (New York: Oxford University Press, 2020), 303.
21. Bird, *The Revolution in Freedoms of Press and Speech,* 303.
22. Wendell Bird, *Criminal Dissent: Prosecutions Under the Alien and Sedition Acts of 1798* (Cambridge, MA: Harvard University Press, 2020), 15.
23. Bird, *The Revolution in Freedoms of Press and Speech,* 334.
24. Wendell Bird, *Press and Speech Under Assault: The Early Supreme Court Justices, the Sedition Act of 1798, and the Campaign Against Dissent* (New York: Oxford University Press, 2016), 312.
25. Bird, *Press and Speech Under Assault,* 199.
26. Bird, *Criminal Dissent,* 207–208.
27. Bird, *Press and Speech Under Assault,* 397.
28. Bird, *Press and Speech Under Assault,* 291.
29. Thomas Cooper, *An Account of the Trial of Thomas Cooper* (Philadelphia: John Bioren, 1800), 2.
30. Bird, *Press and Speech Under Assault,* 291.
31. Cooper, *An Account of the Trial of Thomas Cooper,* 18.
32. Cooper, *An Account of the Trial of Thomas Cooper,* 19.
33. Bird, *Press and Speech Under Assault,* 297.
34. Halperin, *The Alien and Sedition Acts of 1798,* 29.
35. Cooper, *An Account of the Trial of Thomas Cooper,* 35.
36. Bird, *Press and Speech Under Assault,* 297.

37. John Marshall, "Minority Report," in Philip B. Kurland and Ralph Lerner, eds., *The Founders' Constitution* (Indianapolis: Liberty Fund, 1997), 5:138. There is a dispute about whether Marshall authored the "Minority Report," which has also been attributed to Henry Lee. Kurt Lash persuasively argues that Marshall authored the report, and it was only qualms among his biographers in the early years of the twentieth century who began to drop Marshall as the author. Kurt Lash and Alicia Harrison, "Minority Report: John Marshall and the Defense of the Alien and Sedition Acts," 68 *Ohio State Law Journal* 435 (2007).

38. Marshall, "Minority Report," 137.

39. Marshall, "Minority Report," 137.

40. Bird, *Criminal Dissent*, 55–57.

41. Bird, *The Revolution in Freedoms of Press and Speech*, 158. Bird illustrates that there was a much broader British understanding of freedom of speech that existed alongside Blackstone's narrow view of freedom of speech. Bird also shows how in both Britain and America a broader view of free speech emerged over the course of the eighteenth century.

42. James Madison, "Report on the Virginia Resolutions," *The Founders' Constitution*, 5:140.

43. Akhil Reed Amar, *America's Unwritten Constitution* (New York: Basic Books, 2012), x.

44. Madison, "Virginia Report," 141.

45. Bird, *The Revolutions in Freedoms of Press and Speech*, 321.

46. Massachusetts Constitution of 1780, http://press-pubs.uchicago.edu/founders/print_documents/v1ch1s6.html.

47. Bird, *The Revolutions in Freedoms of Press and Speech*, 365, offers a devastating critique of the constitutional historian Leonard Levy's long-standing argument that the only understanding of freedom of speech at the time of the ratification of the First Amendment was Blackstone's. See Leonard Levy, *Emergence of a Free Press* (New York: Oxford University Press, 1985).

48. Bird, *Criminal Dissent*, 117; *The Revolution in Freedoms of the Press and Speech*, 364.

49. James Madison to Thomas Ritchie, September 15, 1821. "I entirely concur in the propriety of resorting to the sense in which the Constitution was accepted and ratified by the nation. In that sense alone it is the legitimate Constitution," Founders Online, https://founders.archives.gov/documents/Madison/04-02-02-0321.

50. Madison, "The Virginia Report," 142.

51. Madison, "The Virginia Report," 142.

52. Bird, *Press and Speech Under Assault,* 275.
53. Bird, *Press and Speech Under Assault,* 277.
54. Bird, *Criminal Dissent,* 7.
55. Bird, *Criminal Dissent,* 94.
56. Cooper, *Account of the Trial of Thomas Cooper,* 30.
57. Halperin, *The Alien and Sedition Act of 1798,* 63.
58. Bird, *Criminal Dissent,* 61.
59. George Thomas, *The Founders and the Idea of a National University: Constituting the American Mind* (New York: Cambridge University Press, 2015), 98–106.
60. Lawrence Lessig, *Fidelity and Constraint: How the Supreme Court Has Read the American Constitution* (New York: Oxford University Press, 2019), 212.
61. *Citizens United v. Federal Election Commission,* 558 U.S. 310 (2010).
62. *Zubik v. Burwell,* 578 U.S. ___ (2016).
63. What Lessig terms fidelity to the judicial role rather than fidelity to constitutional meaning. Lessig, *Fidelity and Constraint,* 212.

Chapter 4

1. "The Great Dissent: Justice Scalia's Opinion in *Morrison v. Olson,*" (video), Federalist Society, October 7, 2018, https://fedsoc.org/commentary/videos/the-great-dissent-justice-scalia-s-opinion-in-morrison-v-olson.
2. *Morrison v. Olson,* 487 U.S. 654, 697–698 (1988) (Scalia, J., dissenting).
3. *Morrison* at 696.
4. *Morrison* at 706.
5. *Morrison* at 703 (Rehnquist, C. J., Opinion of the Court).
6. *Morrison* at 656.
7. *Morrison* at 706 (Scalia, J. dissenting).
8. *Morrison* at 734.
9. Lawrence Lessig, *Fidelity and Constraint: How the Supreme Court Has Read the American Constitution* (New York: Oxford University Press, 2019), 249.
10. Edward A. Purcell, Jr., *Antonin Scalia and American Constitutionalism: The Historical Significance of a Judicial Icon* (New York: Oxford University Press, 2020), 144–150.
11. James Madison, *Federalist* 47, Alexander Hamilton, James Madison, and John Jay, *The Federalist Papers* (New Haven, CT: Yale University Press, 2009), 248.
12. Madison, *Federalist* 37, 182–183.

13. Madison, *Federalist* 47, 247.
14. Jonathan Gienapp, *The Second Creation: Fixing the American Constitution in the Founding Era* (Cambridge, MA: Harvard University Press, 2018), 128.
15. See generally, J. David Alvis, Jeremy Bailey, and Flagg Taylor, *The Contested Removal Power, 1789–2010* (Lawrence: University Press of Kansas, 2013).
16. William Smith, June 17, 1789, House of Representatives, 1st session, *Annals of Congress* (Washington, DC: Gales and Seaton, 1834), 1:527.
17. Smith, June 16, 1789, 1:490.
18. Roger Sherman, June 17, 1789, House of Representatives, 1st session, 1:510.
19. Hamilton, *Federalist* 77, 387.
20. Jeremy Bailey, "The New Unitary Executive and Democratic Theory: The Problem of Alexander Hamilton," 102 *American Political Science Review* 4 (2008), 453–465.
21. James Madison, June 16, 1789, House of Representatives, 1st session, 1:480.
22. Gienapp, *The Second Creation*, 161.
23. Madison, June 16, 1789, 1:481.
24. Jack M. Balkin, *Living Originalism* (Cambridge, MA: Harvard University Press, 2013), 14.
25. Bailey, "Unitary Executive," 461.
26. Madison, June 17, 1789, 1:518.
27. Madison, June 22, 1789, 1: 605. See also, Gienapp, *The Second Creation*, 154.
28. James Madison to Samuel Johnston June 21, 1789. https://oll.libertyfund.org/title/madison-the-writings-vol-5-1787-1790.
29. Madison, Federalist 37, 182. See also William Baude, "Constitutional Liquidation," 71 *Stanford Law Review* 1 (2019) and Jack N. Rakove, *Original Meanings: Politics and Ideas in the Making of the Constitution* (New York: Knopf, 1996), 345–47.
30. Gienapp, *The Second Creation*, 160.
31. *Free Enterprise Fund v. Public Company Accounting Oversight Board*, 561 U.S. 477, 515–516 (2010) (Breyer, J., dissenting).
32. *Free Enterprise Fund* at 516.
33. *Free Enterprise Fund* at 517.
34. *Free Enterprise Fund* at 519.
35. Julian Davis Mortenson, "The Executive Power Clause," 168 *University of Pennsylvania Law Review* 1269 (2020). See also, Julian David Mortenson, "Executive Power Doesn't Mean Much," *The Atlantic*, June 2, 2019.

36. Victoria Nourse, "Reclaiming the Constitutional Text from Originalism: The Case of Executive Power," 106 *California Law Review* 1, 18 (2018).

37. Richard Plides, "Could Congress Simply Codify the DOJ Special Counsel Regulations?," *Lawfare*, August 3, 2017, https://www.lawfareblog.com/could-congress-simply-codify-doj-special-counsel-regulations.

38. *Youngstown Sheet and Tube Co. v. Sawyer*, 343 U.S. 579, 587 (1952).

39. *Youngstown* at 589.

40. Nourse, "Reclaiming the Constitutional Text from Originalism," 18.

41. *Youngstown* at 680 (Vinson, C. J, dissenting).

42. *Hamdi v. Rumsfeld*, 542 U.S. 507 (2004).

43. *Hamdi* at 580 (Thomas, J., dissenting).

44. *Hamdi* at 554 (Scalia, J., dissenting).

45. *Hamdi* at 564.

46. *Zivotofsky v. Kerry*, 576 U.S. 1 (2014).

47. *Zivotofsky* at 32 (Thomas, J., concurring in the judgment/dissenting in part).

48. *Zivotofsky* at 45.

49. *Zivotofsky* at 48.

50. *Zivotofsky* at 84 (Scalia, J., dissenting).

51. *Zivotofsky* at 67.

52. *Zivotofsky* at 74.

53. *Zivotofsky* at 83.

54. Alexander Hamilton, Pacificus 1, *The Pacificus-Helvidius Debates of 1793–1794: Toward the Completion of the American Founding*, ed., Morton J. Frisch (Indianapolis, IN: Liberty Fund, 2007), 13. See also George Thomas, "The Limits of Constitutional Government: Alexander Hamilton on Extraordinary Power and Executive Discretion," in Clement Fatovic and Benjamin A. Kleinerman, eds., *Extra-Legal Power and Legitimacy: Perspectives on Prerogative* (New York: Oxford University Press, 2013), 109.

55. Saikrishna Bangalore Prakash, *Imperial from the Beginning: The Constitution of the Original Executive* (New Haven, CT: Yale University Press, 2015), argues that the president was thought of as monarchical from the beginning. But Prakash also argues that it was a limited and checked monarchy, Saikrishna Bangalore Prakash, *The Living Presidency: An Originalist Argument Against Its Ever-Expanding Powers* (Cambridge, MA: Harvard University Press, 2020). See also, Mortenson, "The Executive Power Clause."

56. Hamilton, Pacificus 1, 13.

57. Hamilton, Pacificus 1, 16.

58. Madison, Helvidius 1, 58.
59. Madison, Helvidius 1, 59.
60. Madison, Hevlidius 1, 64.
61. Madison, Hevlidius 1, 61.

Chapter 5

1. *Goesaert v. Clearly*, 335 U.S. 464, 465 (1948).
2. *Brown v. the Board of Education*, 347 U.S. 483 (1954).
3. *Korematsu v. United States*, 323 U.S. 214 (1944).
4. *Goesaert* at 467 (Rutledge, J., dissenting).
5. *Adkins v. Children's Hospital*, 261 U.S. 526, 556 (1923).
6. *Adkins* at 570 (Holmes, J., dissenting).
7. *Adkins* at 555.
8. Elizabeth Beaumont, *The Civic Constitution: Civic Visions and Struggles in the Path Toward Constitutional Democracy* (New York: Oxford University Press, 2014), 164.
9. *Home Building and Loan Association v. Blaisdell*, 290 U.S. 398, 449 (1934) (Sutherland, J., dissenting).
10. *Lochner v. New York*, 198 U.S. 45, 75 (1905) (Holmes, J., dissenting).
11. Lawrence Lessig, *Fidelity and Constraint: How the Supreme Court Has Read the American Constitution* (New York: Oxford University Press, 2019), 18.
12. Jack M. Balkin, *Living Originalism* (Cambridge, MA: Harvard University Press, 2013), 4.
13. *Adkins* at 553.
14. Beaumont, *The Civic Constitution*, 208–209.
15. *Bradwell v. Illinois*, 83 U.S. 130, 141 (1873).
16. Lessig, *Fidelity and Constraint*, 387.
17. Susan B. Anthony, "Constitutional Argument," *The Elizabeth Cady Stanton-Susan B. Anthony Reader*, ed., Ellen Carol DuBois (Boston: Northeastern University Press, 1992), 158.
18. Ruth Bader Ginsburg, "Brief for the Appellant in *Reed v. Reed* (1971)," Corey Brettschneider, ed., *Decisions and Dissents of Justice Ruth Bader Ginsburg* (New York: Penguin, 2020), 4.
19. David A. Strauss, *The Living Constitution* (New York: Oxford University Press, 210), 113–114.
20. *Missouri v. Holland*, 252 U.S. 416, 433 (1920).
21. J. Harvey Wilkinson III, *Cosmic Constitutional Theory: Why Americans Are Losing Their Inalienable Right to Self-Governance* (New York: Oxford University Press, 2012), 9.

22. Abraham Lincoln, Seventh Lincoln-Douglas Debate, *The Writings of Abraham Lincoln*, ed., Steven B. Smith (New Haven, CT: Yale University Press, 2012), 221.

23. Thomas Jefferson to James Madison, December 20, 1787, Founders Online, https://founders.archives.gov/documents/Jefferson/01-12-02-0454.

24. Ginsburg, "Brief for the Appellant in *Reed v. Reed*, 6."

25. Balkin, *Living Originalism*, 332.

26. For a powerful realist account of democracy, see Christopher H. Achen and Larry Bartels, *Democracy for Realists: Why Elections Do Not Produce Responsive Government* (Princeton, NJ: Princeton University Press, 2016).

27. William Baude, "Is Originalism Our Law?," 115 *Columbia Law Review* 2349, 2380 (2015).

28. *Obergefell v. Hodges*, No. 14-556, transcript of oral argument at page 49 (lines 15-19) and 43 (lines 9-12).

29. *Obergefell v. Hodges*, 576 U.S. ____, 2 (2015) slip opinion (Scalia, J., dissenting).

30. Wilkinson, *Cosmic Constitutional Theory*, 52.

31. *McCulloch v. Maryland*, 17 U.S. 316, 407 (1819).

32. *McCulloch* at 406.

33. *Printz v. United States*, 521 U.S. 898, 919 (1997).

34. Amanda Hollis-Brusky, *Ideas with Consequences: The Federalist Society and the Conservative Counterrevolution* (New York: Oxford University Press, 2014), 130.

35. *Printz* at 947 (Stevens, J., dissenting).

36. *Printz* at 956.

37. *Printz* at 939.

38. Alexander M. Bickel, *The Least Dangerous Branch: The Supreme Court at the Bar of Politics* (New Haven, CT: Yale University Press, 1986).

39. John Hart Ely, *Democracy and Distrust: A Theory of Judicial Review* (Cambridge, MA: Harvard University Press, 1980).

40. *Shelby County v. Holder*, 570 U.S. 529 (2013).

Conclusion

1. James Madison, Federalist 37. In Alexander Hamilton, James Madison, and John Jay, *The Federalist Papers* (New Haven: Yale University Press, 2009), 182-183.

2. *Roberto A. Rucho v. Common Cause*, 588 U.S. ____, 7 (2019) slip opinion (Roberts, C. J., opinion of the Court).

3. *Rucho* at 30 (Roberts, C. J., opinion).

4. *Rucho* at 19 (Roberts, C. J., opinion).

5. *Luther v. Borden*, 48 U.S. 1 (1849) and *Baker v. Carr*, 369 U.S. 186 (1962).

6. *Rucho* at 7, slip opinion (Kagan, J., dissenting).

7. *Rucho* at 15 (Kagan, J., dissenting).

8. *National Federation of Independent Businesses v. Sebelius*, 567 U.S. 519, 573 (2012).

9. *United States v. E.C. Knight*, 156 U.S. 1 (1895).

10. *Carter v. Carter Coal*, 298 U.S. 238 (1936).

11. *NFIB* at 609 (Ginsburg, J., dissenting).

12. Richard H. Fallon, Jr., *The Nature of Constitutional Rights: The Invention and Logic of Strict Judicial Scrutiny* (New York: Cambridge University Press, 2019).

13. *United States v. Carolene Products Co.*, 304 U.S. 144, 152 (1938), footnote 4.

14. Randy Barnett, *Restoring the Lost Constitution: The Presumption of Liberty* (Princeton, NJ: Princeton University Press, 2004).

15. David A. Strauss, *The Living Constitution* (New York: Oxford University Press, 2010).

16. Historians doubt that determining something akin to original public meaning can be done without history because it is key to understanding meaning. See Jack N. Rakove, "Tone Deaf to the Past: More Qualms About Public Meaning Originalism," 84 *Fordham Law Review* 969, 970 (2015).

17. Josh Blackman and Seth Barrett Tillman, "The Emoluments Clauses Litigation, Part 1: The Constitution's Taxonomy of Officers and Offices," *The Volokh Conspiracy, Washington Post*, September 25, 2017, https://www.washingtonpost.com/news/volokh-conspiracy/wp/2017/09/25/the-emoluments-clauses-litigation-part-1-the-constitutions-taxonomy-of-officers-and-offices/.

18. Lawrence Solum, "Legal Theory Lexicon: Corpus Linguistics," *Legal Theory Blog,* January 13, 2019, https://lsolum.typepad.com/legaltheory/2019/01/legal-theory-lexicon-corpus-linguistics.html.

19. Jack N. Rakove, *Original Meanings: Politics and Ideas in the Making of the Constitution* (New York: Knopf, 1996), 10.

20. *District of Columbia v. Heller*, 554 U.S. 570 (2008).

21. Jamal Greene, "Heller High Water? The Future of Originalism," 3 *Harvard Journal of Law and Public Policy* 326, 336 (2009).

22. Keith E. Whittington, *Constitutional Interpretation: Textual Meaning, Original Intent, and Judicial Review* (Lawrence: University Press of Kansas, 1999), 10–11.

23. Barnett, *Restoring the Lost Constitution*, 120.
24. Jack M. Balkin, *Living Originalism* (Cambridge, MA: Harvard University Press, 2013), 259.
25. Keith E. Whittington, "On Pluralism Within Originalism," in Grant Hustcroft and Bradley W. Miller, eds., *The Challenge of Originalism: Theories of Constitutional Interpretation* (New York: Cambridge University Press, 2011), 80.
26. Balkin, *Living Originalism*, 261.
27. David Robertson, *The Judge as Political Theorist: Contemporary Constitutional Review* (Princeton, NJ: Princeton University Press, 2010), 33.
28. Sanford Levinson, *Framed: Americas 51 Constitutions and the Crisis of Governance* (New York: Oxford University Press, 2012). Levinson distinguishes between the "constitution of settlement" and the "constitutional of contestation."
29. Aharon Barak, *Purposive Interpretation in Law* (Princeton, NJ: Princeton University Press, 2007), 274.
30. As Laurence Tribe puts it in his comment on Scalia's *A Matter of Interpretation*, "In choosing among these views of what counts as 'the Constitution' . . . one must of necessity look outside the Constitution itself." Tribe, Comment, Scalia, *A Matter of Interpretation* (Princeton, NJ: Princeton University Press, 2018), 76.
31. Chris Green, "Is the Oath Argument for Originalism Circular?," *The Originalism Blog*, May 15, 2020, https://originalismblog.typepad.com/the-originalism-blog/2020/05/is-the-oath-argument-for-originalism-circular.html.
32. Jonathan Gienapp, "The Myth of the Constitutional Given: Enumeration and National Power at the Founding," 69 *American University Law Review Forum* 183, 197 (2020).
33. Thomas C. Grey, "The Constitution as Scripture," 37 *Stanford Law Review* 1 (1984).
34. Brett M. Kavanaugh, "Our Anchor for 225 Years and Counting: The Enduring Significance of the Precise Text of the Constitution," 89 *Notre Dame Law Review* 1907, 1909 (2014).
35. George Thomas, *The Madisonian Constitution* (Baltimore: Johns Hopkins University Press, 2008), 17–19.
36. Ronald Dworkin, *Justice in Robes* (Cambridge, MA: Harvard University Press, 2006), 125.
37. Ronald Dworkin, *Freedom's Law: The Moral Reading of the American Constitution* (Cambridge, MA: Harvard University Press, 1996), 10.

38. Dworkin, *Freedom's Law*, 2.

39. Michael McConnell, "The Importance of Humility in Judicial Review: A Comment on Ronald Dworkin's 'Moral Reading' of the Constitution," 65 *Fordham Law Review* 1280, 1284 (1997).

40. J. Harvey Wilkinson III, *Cosmic Constitutional Theory: Why Americans Are Losing Their Inalienable Right to Self-Governance* (New York: Oxford University Press, 2012).

Index

For the benefit of digital users, indexed terms that span two pages (e.g., 52–53) may, on occasion, appear on only one of those pages.